Grokking
Relational
Database
Design

Qiang Hao
Michail Tsikerdekis

MANNING
SHELTER ISLAND

··

To our family and friends, for their endless support and encouragement.
And to all those who believe in the power of curiosity and persistence,
may this book serve as a companion on your journey of learning.

brief contents

contents

Part 1 Get started 1

preface

For years, we have taught courses on database management systems, and one recurring challenge we've noticed is the overwhelming difficulty students have with conventional textbooks. These materials, while comprehensive, often feel tedious and painful for students to chew through, making the learning process more daunting than it needs to be.

Our teaching experiences led us to envision a different kind of resource—one that makes the principles of relational database design more approachable and engaging. That opportunity came when Dr. Daniel Zingaro, an editor at Manning and a colleague from the University of Toronto Mississauga, reached out to us. Daniel asked whether we would be interested in writing a book that could bring these concepts to life in a way that learners could better grasp and enjoy.

The result is *Grokking Relational Database Design*, a book that focuses not just on the technicalities but also on how to teach them effectively, emphasizing clarity, real-world relevance, and a step-by-step approach. Whether you're new to the field or seeking a refresher on concepts you learned years ago, this book is designed for you.

In today's world, where AI and machine learning are rapidly transforming industries, the role of relational databases remains fundamental. Although new technologies such as NoSQL databases and Big Data solutions have emerged, relational databases continue to be the backbone of data storage, especially in environments that require structured, reliable, scalable data solutions. Moreover, the rise of AI and machine learning has only increased the demand for clean, organized data—something that relational databases excel at providing. By mastering relational database design, you'll not only gain a crucial skill but also position yourself to harness the full potential of

AI and machine learning, ensuring the integrity and accessibility of the data that powers these technologies.

We hope that this book becomes a valuable resource for anyone venturing into this critical area of technology and helps bridge the gap between foundational database principles and their applications in the rapidly evolving tech landscape.

acknowledgments

We would like to sincerely thank the following people for their invaluable contributions to this book:

- *Cody Pham*—Cody created all the illustrations for this book. His vivid visuals greatly enhance its readability, making complex concepts easier to grasp.

- *Dr. Daniel Zingaro*—Dr. Zingaro was instrumental in helping us define the scope of the book. He offered insightful guidance on structuring the content across chapters.

- *Elesha Hyde*—Elesha provided invaluable support through her detailed suggestions and feedback, which were essential to the editing process.

- *Louis Davidson*—Louis offered insightful suggestions and feedback that strengthened the robustness and clarity of each chapter.

- *Jonathan Gennick*—Jonathan contributed useful suggestions to the revision of this book.

- *The team at Manning Publications*—We are grateful to the team at Manning for their expertise and dedication in helping bring this book to life.

- *All the reviewers who took the time to provide their valuable feedback*—David Spenn, Ganesh Falak, Ganesh Swaminathan, Grant Colley, Heng Zhang, Jim Amrhein, José Alberto Reyes Quevedo, Marcus Geselle, Maxim Volgin, Nadir Doctor, Oliver Korten, Orlando Méndez Morales, Patrick Regan, Peter A. Schott, Potito Coluccelli, Radhakrishna MV, Sasha Sankova, Trevoir Williams, Valerie Parham-Thompson, Víctor Durán, Vojta Tuma, William Jamir Silva, and Yilun Zhang. Your suggestions helped improve the book.

about this book

Grokking Relational Database Design teaches the art of database design through hands-on projects, insightful illustrations, and practical, action-oriented learning. Unlike many introductory books that focus primarily on SQL syntax and formal database theory, this book emphasizes a foundational approach to relational design thinking. You'll learn how to structure databases from the ground up, creating systems that are both efficient and intuitive—databases that stand the test of time and are a pleasure to work with long after they're built.

Who should read this book?

This book is written primarily for those who are new to database design or are seeking a refresher on concepts they may have learned years ago. Each chapter is crafted to be both accessible and thorough, providing practical guidance on every key concept essential to designing effective relational databases.

How this book is organized: A road map

This book is organized in three parts covering eight chapters:

- *Part 1, Get started*—The first part introduces the essentials. In chapters 1 and 2, you gain foundational knowledge of Structured Query Language (SQL), which is essential for effective database design. Chapter 3 provides a comprehensive overview of the principles and processes that define successful database design.

- *Part 2, Master database design*—Spanning four chapters, this part delves into the core skills needed to excel at database design:
  - *Entities and attributes*—Learn how to identify and define entities and their attributes based on requirements analysis, laying the groundwork for a well-structured database.
  - *Relationships*—Discover how to establish meaningful relationships among entities, guided by design principles that ensure consistency and usability.
  - *Normalization and implementation*—Explore the process of normalizing your design to minimize data anomalies during insertion, updates, and deletions. You'll also learn how to translate your design into SQL code, bringing your database to life.
  - *Security and optimization*—Gain practical insights into securing and optimizing your database, addressing performance, and protecting data integrity.
- *Part 3, Database design and AI*—In this final part, you see how generative AI can accelerate the design process, helping you streamline workflows and enhance efficiency in database design. You walk through the full process of designing a database from scratch with the help of ChatGPT.

About the code

You can get executable snippets of code from the liveBook (online) version of this book at https://livebook.manning.com/book/grokking-relational-database-design. The complete code for the examples in the book is available for download from the Manning website at www.manning.com and from GitHub at https://github.com/Neo-Hao/grokking-relational-database-design. Each chapter has a dedicated folder in the repository, where you'll find scripts and step-by-step instructions that align with the content of that chapter.

liveBook discussion forum

Purchase of *Grokking Relational Database Design* includes free access to liveBook, Manning's online reading platform. Using liveBook's exclusive discussion features, you can attach comments to the book globally or to specific sections or paragraphs. It's a snap to make notes for yourself, ask and answer technical questions, and receive help from the authors and other users. To access the forum, go to https://livebook.manning.com/ book/grokking-relational-database-design/discussion. You can also learn more about Manning's forums and the rules of conduct at https://livebook.manning.com/discussion.

Manning's commitment to our readers is to provide a venue where meaningful dialogue between individual readers and between readers and authors can take place. It is not a commitment to any specific amount of participation on the part of the authors, whose contributions to the forum remain voluntary (and unpaid). We suggest you try asking the authors some challenging questions lest their interest stray! The forum and the archives of previous discussions will be accessible on the publisher's website as long as the book is in print.

about the authors

DR. QIANG HAO is an Associate Professor of Computer Science at Western Washington University. His research in computing education is widely recognized and cited within the academic community. Dr. Hao has extensive experience teaching a broad range of courses, such as database systems, data structures, and mobile development. His innovative approach to teaching has earned him high praise from both students and colleagues.

DR. MICHAIL TSIKERDEKIS is an Associate Professor of Computer Science at Western Washington University. His research in cybersecurity has been featured in many top-tier journals and conferences. Over the years, he has taught a variety of courses in various departments such as computer science, information science, and sociology, including database systems and database concepts. He is an IEEE Senior Member and a 24/25 U.S. Fulbright Scholar.

Part 1
Get started

Welcome to the journey into relational database design! In this part, you'll gain foundational skills in Structured Query Language (SQL) that are essential for designing efficient and effective databases. By mastering these basics, you'll be prepared to tackle advanced database concepts with confidence. This part is the "laying the foundation before building the structure" phase. Whether you're new to SQL or need a refresher, this section will guide you through the essentials.

Chapter 1 begins with the basics of SQL that you need for database design. Think of this chapter as your "Hello, World!" moment in database exploration; you'll write your first SQL queries and begin interacting with data in meaningful ways.

Chapter 2 dives a bit deeper into SQL by focusing on expressing the relationships between tables. By the end, you'll have everything you need to use SQL for database design.

Chapter 3 offers a bird's-eye view of database design. You'll explore the full process of good database design and what matters at each step.

Prepare your tool—a notepad, laptop, or database application—and settle into a focused space. Let's dive into the exciting world of relational database design!

In this chapter

- You get a foundation for the rest of the book.

- You learn the basics of relational databases.

- You peek into database design.

- You write your first SQL query and learn more about the basics of SQL.

What you need to know

As you read this chapter, you will find some code snippets. If you want to execute those code snippets or see what changes need to be made to the code for different relational database management systems (RDBMSs), check the GitHub repository that accompanies this book (https://github.com/Neo-Hao/grokking-relational-database-design). You can find the scripts for this chapter in the `chapter_01` folder; follow the instructions in the `README.md` file to run the scripts.

Overview

Database design is a critical yet easily neglected step in software development. Nearly every application requires data storage and management to some extent, but not every application has a well-designed database. If you design a database without knowing the principles of effective database design, your application may suffer from problems you weren't expecting, such as disorganized data or queries that take too long and too many resources to run. These problems can lead to bugs and a bad user experience.

By contrast, effective database design can serve as a solid foundation for effective software development. Effective database design makes sure that an application's data is well organized and structured, which in turn supports efficient data querying and manipulation that contributes to solid applications and superior user experience. Regardless of where you are in your journey of learning programming and software development, it is essential to learn how to design databases effectively and possibly how to talk to nontech people without making their eyes glaze over with boredom as well.

This book covers how to design databases and assumes no previous knowledge of databases or programming. By the end of this book, you will have a good understanding of how to design relational databases from scratch. We aim to help you achieve this goal via down-to-earth definitions and explanations, rich examples, and active learning practice.

This chapter aims to introduce relational databases, define a set of terms that you will see in the next few chapters, and cover the basics of *Structured Query Language* (SQL). SQL (often pronounced "sequel") is the programming language used to manage data in relational databases, and it's essential for you to have some understanding of SQL to have a robust understanding of database design.

Relational databases

Once upon a time, a small company used Microsoft Excel spreadsheets to store all its customer data. At first, everything seemed to run smoothly, and the company was able to access and update the data as needed. As time went on, the company grew and acquired more customers, and the spreadsheets became increasingly more difficult to manage. There were duplicates and inconsistencies in the data, and the spreadsheets became so large and unwieldy that they took a long time to load and update.

One day, the company received a call from a customer who was charged twice for a single purchase. When the company tried to access the customer's data in a spreadsheet to investigate the problem, they found that the data had been corrupted and was no longer accessible. As more and more customers began to report similar problems, the company learned the hard way that spreadsheets are a bad choice for storing customer data. The company eventually invested in a relational database system that could handle the scale of its data and ensure the integrity of its records.

If you have a very small amount of data with a simple structure to store, a spreadsheet can get the job done; you don't need a database at all. However, as data complexity and volume increase, you probably should think again. When you need to apply access control to the data, maintain its consistency, integrity, and scalability, and conduct routine data analysis, you absolutely need a database.

Relational databases have been, and still are, the default technology for storing and accessing data when scale, data consistency, and data integrity are all required. In recent years, machine learning and AI have helped sustain and even boost the popularity of relational databases. In this section, you will learn some fundamental concepts of relational databases, such as tables, entities, and RDBMS.

Tables, entities, and primary keys

A *relational database* is a collection of tables that store data. A table is like a spreadsheet, which you are likely familiar with. Just like a spreadsheet, the data in a table is organized into rows and columns. A table can be used to represent an entity or a relationship between entities, with each row representing a single data record of that entity and each column representing an attribute of that entity.

What is an entity? An *entity* is an object or concept that can be described by many attributes. Suppose that we are running an online store called The Sci-Fi Collective that sells sci-fi products (such as a time machine that takes you back only 5 minutes, in case you forgot your keys). Products sold by The Sci-Fi Collective are entities, and each can be described by at least four attributes: name, description, price, and manufacturer. When we map products to a table in the database supporting the online store of The Sci-Fi Collective, the four attributes will be mapped to four individual columns, and each product will be represented as a row in this table.

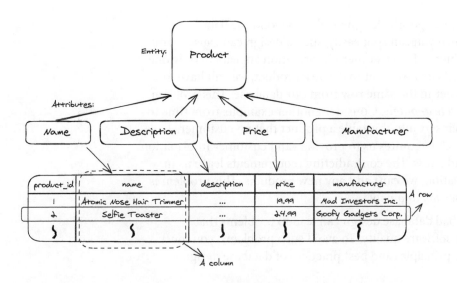

In addition to the four columns, you may notice that we added another column, `product_id`, in the preceding table. All values in the `product_id` column are unique and can be used to identify an individual row. We call `product_id` the *primary key* of the `product` table. Think of the primary key as the "one ring to rule them all": each table can have only one to uniquely identify its rows. You can find a much deeper discussion of primary keys in chapter 4.

It is not uncommon for one spreadsheet to store the information of multiple entities. You may wonder whether to do the same with tables in a relational database. If we decide to store the information of customers and products in one table for The Sci-Fi Collective, for example, the table will look like this:

product_id	name	price	manufacturer	customer_id	customer_name	customer_email	quantity
1	Atomic Nose ...	19.99	Mad Inventors Inc.	a1	Bob	bob@gmail.com	5
2	Selfie Toaster	24.99	Goofy Gadgets Corp.	b2	Dave	dave@outlook.com	15
3	Cat-Poop Coffee	29.99	Absurd Accessories	a1	Bob	bob@gmail.com	2
...	...	...	...	...	...	...	...
9	The Infinite ...	9.99	Silly Supplies Co.	j8	John	john@123.net	1
10	The Neuralyzer	33.55	Silly Supplies Co.	p9	Katy	katy@123.net	2

This table is a typical poorly designed table. Beyond the data redundancy, which you can spot easily, such a design can cause many unexpected problems. If a customer's information appears in only one row, for example, when we want to delete a product, we will have to delete the customer in the same row from our database. This problem is known as a *delete anomaly*. Consider another example: from time to time we need to insert into this table a product that no customers have bought, but the table requires us to provide valid customer information whenever we add a row. The contradicting requirements leave us in an awkward situation; we can't add any new products. This problem is known as an *insertion anomaly*.

As you can see, bad database design can lead to problems that negatively affect software quality. To avoid such problems, you must master the basic principles and best practices of database design.

Relational database management systems and SQL

Relational databases and tables rely on the help of RDBMS to physically store and manage the data. Edgar Codd at IBM developed the first RDBMS in the 1970s.

An *RDBMS* is software that interacts with the underlying hardware and operating system to physically store and manage data in relational databases. Additionally, an RDBMS provides tools to create, modify, and query databases along with other important functions such as security controls. You may be familiar with some commonly used RDBMS, such as MySQL, MariaDB, PostgreSQL, and SQLite. When you need to deploy a database that you designed, you will need to interact with one of the available RDBMS on the market.

One of the most notable tools that nearly all RDBMSs support is SQL, a programming language that you can use to create, modify, and query data stored in tables in an RDBMS. Although different RDBMS vendors may implement their own variations and extensions, SQL has been standardized over the years.

As a result, the consistency of SQL among RDBMSs is high, and the variations don't matter much in the context of this book.

Because this book is primarily a database design book, of course, SQL may seem less important. Database design doesn't necessarily require you to use SQL. Some RDBMS comes with graphical tools to generate SQL scripts that automatically create databases and tables based on your design. But having some understanding of SQL can make it easier to learn database design, especially when it relates to structural or design problems such as data integrity, optimization, and scalability. After all, SQL is a standardized language that most RDBMSs use, so knowing SQL will allow you to rely less on graphical tools and work with different types of RDBMSs. We will cover the basics of SQL in this chapter and in chapter 2.

Your first SQL query

In this section, you will learn SQL by executing your first SQL query. We will use the example that you saw in the preceding section, the database of The Sci-Fi Collective (because who doesn't like sci-fi stuff?). The database contains many tables, but the `product` table is all you need to focus on for now. The `product` table looks like the following:

product_id	name	description	price	manufacturer
1	Atomic Nose Hair Trimmer	...	19.99	Mad Inventors Inc.
2	Selfie Toaster	...	24.99	Goofy Gadgets Corp.
3	Cat-Poop Coffee	...	29.99	Absurd Accessories
...	...		...	...
9	The Infinite Improbability Generator	...	9.99	Silly Supplies Co.
10	The Neuralyzer	...	33.55	Silly Supplies Co.

First, you will load a prepared SQL script to generate a database and this table. We prepared the SQL scripts that generate this table with

data, which you can find in our GitHub repository (https://github.com/
Neo-Hao/grokking-relational-database-design). You can follow the
instructions of the `README.md` file in the `chapter_01` folder to execute
the prepared script for your preferred RDBMS or tool. The easiest
approach is to use SQLite Online, as follows:

1. Clone or download our GitHub repository (https://github.com/Neo-
   Hao/grokking-relational-database-design).
2. Navigate to SQLite Online (https://sqliteonline.com).
3. Choose your target RDBMS in the left sidebar, and click the Click
   button to Connect.
4. Click Import, and load the script corresponding to your chosen
   RDBMS (such as `mysql_db.sql` from the downloaded or cloned
   GitHub repository for MariaDB).
5. Click Okay.

After that, you will be ready to query the `product` table. You can type
the following query (as a whole) into the code editor on SQLite Online
and then click Run:

```
SELECT name
FROM product
WHERE price > 20;
```

What does this query do? The `price > 20` part may be a dead giveaway.
The query retrieves the names of products whose prices are higher
than `20`. We know that there are 10 rows representing 10 products
in the `product` table and that 5 products (such as Atomic Nose Hair
Trimmer) sell at a price below `20`, so the names of the other 5 products
are returned. Your result should look like this:

You may notice that this SQL query has a lot of similarities to plain English. The reason is that SQL is special. You see, most programming languages are imperative. Coding with an *imperative* language, such as Java or Python, requires you to specify both what to do and how to do it. SQL, however, is *declarative*, which means that you need to specify only what to do. The steps required to carry out the task are SQL's job to figure out. Specifying what you want instead of how to get it done is more natural for human beings, and that's why SQL resembles plain English.

To be specific, SQL is like English, with little to no small talk. But you don't have the same freedom in word choices when it comes to putting together a SQL query. You must use a set of SQL clauses (also known as *statements*) and follow some rules. In your first query, you used the following three clauses:

- SELECT—The SELECT clause allows you to specify the columns you want to retrieve from a table. In your first query, you only asked for the name column; thus, the SELECT statement was SELECT name.
- FROM—The FROM clause specifies the source you want to retrieve data from one or more tables. In your first query, you asked only for data from the product table; thus, the FROM clause was FROM product.
- WHERE—The WHERE clause allows you to specify conditions to filter the data retrieved by the SELECT clause. In your first query, you want only the names of those products whose prices are higher than 20; thus, the query was SELECT name FROM product WHERE price > 20;.

When you finish a SQL query, you should use a semicolon (;) to indicate its end. The semicolon tells the RDBMS that this is the end of a SQL query and that anything after it belongs to a new query.

The basics of SQL queries

Our preferred approach for learning SQL is to grasp the most important clauses and learn the rest only when necessary. Although SQL has many clauses, they are not equally important. The most important ones can help you build a solid foundation, as well as construct a mental map that can guide your future learning.

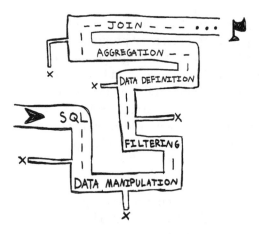

Therefore, instead of trying to cover every SQL clause, we will cover only the ones that are essential or critical to your future learning. In this chapter, you will learn important clauses that you can use to query a single table.

Filtering

Filtering is a common data retrieval task. Whenever you need only a subset of data that meets some criteria, you need the help of the WHERE clause to filter the data.

From your first SQL query, you know that the WHERE clause is followed by the criteria you want to use to filter the data. The following query, for example, retrieves the names and descriptions of products whose prices are lower than 30 from the product table:

```
SELECT name, description
FROM product
WHERE price < 30;
```

When you want to retrieve more than one column, you can list all of them after the SELECT keyword and separate them with commas.

What if we want to retrieve only the products that come from a specific manufacturer, such as Mad Inventors Inc.? We can achieve this via the following query:

```
SELECT name
FROM product
WHERE manufacturer = 'Mad Inventors Inc.';
```

This query yields the following result:

name
Atomic Nose Hair Trimmer
The Mind Probe
Lightsabers

In the preceding query, the operator that checks equality is a single equal sign (=). Additionally, you may notice that the manufacturer name is wrapped in single quotes (' '), indicating a string data type. Does SQL have different data types? Yes. SQL data can be broadly divided into six categories:

- Numeric data types (such as `INT`)
- String data types (such as `TEXT`)
- Date or time data types (such as `DATE`)
- Unicode character string data types (such as `VARCHAR`)
- Binary data types (such as `BINARY`)
- Miscellaneous data types (such as `XML`)

In the `product` table, the data type of the `manufacturer` column is string. By contrast, the `price` column is numeric.

Now that you know how to filter both numeric and string data, you can create one filter that combines the two criteria by using logical operators. `AND` and `OR` are the two most frequently used logical operators. The `AND` operator means the same as it does in plain English; the same can be said of `OR`. We can combine two individual criteria using `AND`, as follows:

```
SELECT *
FROM product
WHERE price < 30 AND
manufacturer = 'Mad Inventors Inc.';
```

This query yields the following result:

product_id	name	description	price	manufacturer
1	Atomic Nose Hair Trimmer	...	19.99	Mad Inventors Inc.
6	The Mind Probe	...	19.99	Mad Inventors Inc.
7	Lightsabers	...	25.00	Mad Inventors Inc.

Unlike previous queries, this query retrieves every column from the
product table. The star (*) following the SELECT keyword indicates
all columns. The combination of the two filtering criteria retrieves all
columns of only the products that are manufactured by Mad Inventors
Inc. and have a price below 30.

Aggregation

Aggregation, an important task in SQL, involves performing
calculations on a set of rows to produce a single result. By aggregating
data, you can gain insights into trends and patterns in the data that may
not be visible at the individual record level. The most frequently used
aggregate functions are

- COUNT() — Counts the number of rows
- SUM() — Calculates the sum of values in a numeric column
- AVG() — Calculates the average value in a numeric column
- MAX() — Finds the maximum value in a column
- MIN() — Finds the minimum value in a column

When we formulate a SQL query that involves aggregation, we should
place the aggregate function in the SELECT statement. We can count the
number of rows in the product table this way:

```
SELECT COUNT(*) FROM product;
```

This query yields the following result:

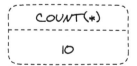

COUNT(*)
10

You may notice that the column name is the same as the aggregate function command. If you are dealing with an RDBMS other than MariaDB, the column name may be COUNT() or something else. If you don't like the default column name, you can provide a more readable one by using an alias via the AS clause. You can calculate the average price of all products that are sold in the store and use avg_price as the column name, as in this example:

```
SELECT AVG(price) AS avg_price
FROM product
WHERE manufacturer = 'Mad Inventors Inc.';
```

This query yields the following result, in which the column name is avg_ price and the only value is the average of all product prices in the table:

avg_price
21.66

In both examples, you applied aggregate functions to all rows in a table. You can also apply aggregate functions to multiple groups of rows in a table. Sometimes, you need to group the data by one or more columns and analyze the grouped data. You can group data via the GROUP BY clause, which is commonly used in combination with aggregate functions. The GROUP BY clause is always followed by one or more attribute names separated by commas. You can count the number of products per manufacturer like this:

```
SELECT COUNT(*) AS product_count, manufacturer
FROM product
GROUP BY manufacturer;
```

This query yields the following result, possibly in varying order:

product_count	manufacturer
2	Absurd Accessories
1	Goofy Gadgets Corp.
3	Mad Inventors Inc.
3	Silly Supplies Co.
1	Wacky Wares Ltd.

As another example, you can calculate the average price of products per manufacturer:

```
SELECT AVG(price) AS avg_price, manufacturer
FROM product
GROUP BY manufacturer;
```

This query yields the following result:

avg_price	manufacturer
22.5449...	Absurd Accessories
24.99	Goofy Gadgets Corp.
21.659...	Mad Inventors Inc.
17.843...	Silly Supplies Co.
39.99	Wacky Wares Ltd.

When you use aggregate functions with the GROUP BY clause, you need to include the attributes following the GROUP BY clause in the SELECT statement. Otherwise, the results may not make much sense. The following query groups the data by the manufacturer column but doesn't include it in the SELECT statement:

```
--comment: will yield something difficult to interpret
SELECT COUNT(*) AS product_count
FROM product
GROUP BY manufacturer;
```

The result will be much harder to chew because you see only a column of numbers and have no idea what the numbers stand for:

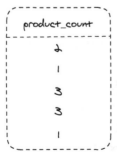

product_count
2
1
3
3
1

As another example, the following query calculates the average product price per manufacturer but doesn't include the manufacturer column in the SELECT statement:

```
--comment: will yield something difficult to interpret
SELECT AVG(price) AS avg_price
FROM product
GROUP BY manufacturer;
```

As in the last example, the result is difficult to interpret because you see only a column of decimals and have no idea what they stand for:

More important, you should exclude from the SELECT statement any columns that are not in the GROUP BY clause unless they are used with aggregate functions. The following query attempts to count the number of products per manufacturer, but the name column in the SELECT statement is neither in the GROUP BY clause nor used with an aggregate function:

```
-- comment: will either lead to an error
-- comment: or yield a misleading result
SELECT COUNT(*) AS product_count, manufacturer, name
FROM product
GROUP BY manufacturer;
```

A query like this one leads to errors or yields a misleading result, depending on the RDBMS you use. PostgreSQL, for example, will make the following complaint:

```
ERROR: column "product.name" must appear
in the GROUP BY clause or be used in
an aggregate function
```

SQLite yields a misleading result without complaint:

product_number	manufacturer	name
2	Absurd Accessories	Cat-Poop Coffee
1	Goofy Gadgets Corp.	Selfie Toaster
3	Mad Inventors Inc.	Atomic Nose Hair Trimmer
3	Silly Supplies Co.	Unicorn Hair Polish
1	Wacky Wares Ltd.	Inflatable Briefcase

If you check all 10 products in the product table, you see that there is only 1 Atomic Nose Hair Trimmer instead of 3. But because the query doesn't know how to deal with the name column, it simply shows the name value in the first row it encounters per group.

As another example, the following query attempts to calculate the average price of products per manufacturer, but the product_id column in the SELECT statement is not in the GROUP BY clause:

```
-- comment: will either lead to an error
-- comment: or yield a misleading result
SELECT product_id, AVG(price) AS avg_price, manufacturer
FROM product
GROUP BY manufacturer;
```

Depending on the RDBMS you use, you may get either an error or a misleading result. PostgreSQL, for example, will make the following complaint:

```
ERROR: column "product.product_id" must appear
in the GROUP BY clause or be used in an
aggregate function
```

SQLite will yield a misleading result without complaint:

product_id	avg_price	manufacturer
3	22.5449...	Absurd Accessories
2	24.99	Goofy Gadgets Corp.
1	21.659...	Mad Inventors Inc.
5	17.843...	Silly Supplies Co.
4	39.99	Wacky Wares Ltd.

If you check the third row of the `product` table, you will see that its price is `29.99` instead of `22.5449…`. The preceding aggregated result is obviously wrong. Because this query doesn't know how to deal with the `product_id` column, it simply shows the first `product_id` value it encounters per manufacturer group.

In summary, when you use aggregate functions with the GROUP BY clause, you need to be careful about what attributes to include in the SELECT statement. The SELECT statement should contain only those nonaggregate attributes that show up in the GROUP BY clause. *Nonaggregate attributes* are attributes that are not involved in aggregation.

Table and data management

You've worked with SQL on a table that we gave you, but sometimes, you need to make your own tables and to manage those tables and their data.

Table and data management are important tasks in SQL. The SQL commands dedicated to such tasks are commonly known as *data definition language* (DDL). By contrast, the SQL clauses and statements you saw in previous sections are known as *data manipulation language*. Understanding some DDL is particularly useful for database design.

In this section, you will learn three common table management tasks: creating, altering, and deleting a table. You will also learn how to add data to a new table.

Create tables and add data to tables

You will learn how to create a table and add data to it from the prepared scripts that accompany this chapter. The scripts (such as `mysql_db.sql` for MySQL or MariaDB) aim to create the `product` table for the database supporting The Sci-Fi Collective and populate it with a set of sample data. The `product` table is created with the following command:

```
CREATE TABLE product (
  product_id INT PRIMARY KEY,
  name TEXT NOT NULL,
  description TEXT NOT NULL,
  price DECIMAL(5, 2) NOT NULL,
  manufacturer TEXT NOT NULL
);
```

We need to answer two questions about the command that creates the `product` table:

- What is the general syntax for creating a table?
- What do the different keywords do in this query example?

SQL drama: When your tables throw a fit over duplications

If you have followed along and imported the given SQL script in previous sections, you will see some complaints from SQL when you try to run the following `CREATE TABLE` command.

Why? You ran the same command when you imported the given SQL script in the section "Your first SQL query," which creates a table named `product`. The same RDBMS can't have two tables with the same name. The same can be said of the data insertion commands that will be covered next. A table can't have two identical rows, especially not two rows with the same primary key.

If you want to run the `CREATE TABLE` and data insertion commands covered in this section after importing the prepared scripts, you can do the following:

- If you are using SQLite Online, you can easily reset everything by refreshing the browser tab.

- If you are using an RDBMS running locally or on a server, you need to delete that corresponding table first. You will learn more about deleting and altering tables in this section.

What is the general syntax for creating a table? To create a table, you need the help of the CREATE TABLE command. The syntax of the CREATE TABLE command is as follows:

```
CREATE TABLE table_name (
  column1_name datatype [optional_parameters],
  column2_name datatype [optional_parameters],
  ...
  columnN_name datatype [optional_parameters],
  PRIMARY KEY (columnX_name)
);
```

The definition of the primary key can also be part of the definition of a column, as you saw in the product table example. Unlike optional parameters, the primary key is required in every table.

What do the different keywords do in this query example? First, we specified the table name as product and defined five columns:

- product_id—A numeric data type (INT)
- name—A string data type (TEXT)
- description—A string data type (TEXT)
- price—A numeric data type (DECIMAL)
- manufacturer—A string data type (TEXT)

INT indicates integer, and TEXT indicates string. The only data type worth explaining here is probably DECIMAL. DECIMAL, as a numeric data type, accepts two parameters. The first parameter defines the total number of digits, and the second one defines the number of digits to the right of the decimal point. We use DECIMAL(5,2), for example, to define the price attribute to allow five digits in total and two digits to the right of the decimal point.

In addition to the data types, you may notice that we specified every attribute as NOT NULL. In SQL, a NULL value represents an unknown value. Similar to when you're trying to remember someone's name and it's on the tip of your tongue, the value is either missing or unknown. Allowing NULL values for attributes may lead SQL to have unexpected behaviors. When you add 10 and a NULL value, for example, you end up with a NULL value; the sum of an unknown value and 10 is still unknown. When you do calculations on NULL values, all the results may end up as NULL.

Last, the PRIMARY KEY definition was used to specify which attribute we want to use as the primary key for this table. The attribute name needs to be placed in parentheses following the PRIMARY KEY definition.

When the product table is created in a database, it is ready for you to add data to it. To add data to a table, you need help from the INSERT INTO command. The INSERT INTO command allows you to insert one or more rows of data into a table. Here's its basic syntax:

```
INSERT INTO table_name (column1, column2, ...)
VALUES (value1, value2, ...);
```

In the same script, you can find an example of adding data to the product table. You can insert a single row into the table as follows:

```
INSERT INTO product (product_id, name, description,
price, manufacturer)
VALUES (
  1,
  'Atomic Nose Hair Trimmer',
  'Trim your nose hairs... of an atomic clock!',
  19.99,
  'Mad Inventors Inc.'
);
```

Or you can insert multiple rows of data into the table:

```
INSERT INTO product
  (product_id, name, description, price, manufacturer)
VALUES
(
  2,
  'Selfie Toaster',
  'Get your face on... with our selfie toaster',
  24.99,
  'Goofy Gadgets Corp.'
),
  (
  3,
  'Cat-Poop Coffee',
  'The only coffee... the finest cat poop ...',
  29.99,
  'Absurd Accessories'
);
```

Alter and drop tables

From time to time, you may need to alter or drop an existing table because—let's face it—sometimes you need to rearrange the furniture in your data house.

There are many ways to alter a table, such as adding a column, modifying the data type of a column, or renaming the entire table. You can rely on the help of the ALTER TABLE command to perform all these tasks. If you want to add another column representing serial numbers to the product table, for example, you can use the following query:

```
ALTER TABLE product
ADD serial_number INT;
```

When the preceding query gets executed, a new column named serial_number is added to this table, and its data type is integer. When you realize that integer is not the best data type for serial numbers, you may update its data type to string via the following query:

```
-- comment: SQLite doesn't support altering
-- comment: a column's data type directly
ALTER TABLE product
ALTER COLUMN serial_number TEXT;
```

Although you have many ways to alter a table, there's only one way to drop a table. To do so, you need the `DROP TABLE` command followed by the name of the table you want to drop. If you intend to drop the `product` table, for example, you can use the following query:

```
DROP TABLE_product;
```

You need to be careful when using the `DROP TABLE` command because it will permanently delete the table and all its data.

This section doesn't aim to be an exhaustive list of all commands for altering or dropping a table. If you want to know more, please check out the SQL manual or your target RDBMS. That said, you have taken an important step toward mastering databases and database design. The things you've achieved in this chapter will propel your learning throughout the rest of the book—small choices that may cascade into a design masterpiece worthy of being displayed in a tech gala one day, should they ever become reality.

Recap

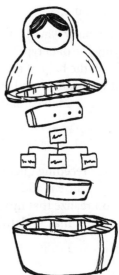

- A relational database is a collection of tables that store data.
- A table is used to represent an entity or a relationship between entities in a database.
- An entity is an object or concept that can be described by many attributes.
- An RDBMS is software that interacts with the underlying hardware and operating system to physically store and manage data in relational databases.
- Filtering data requires help from at least three SQL clauses: `SELECT`, `FROM`, and `WHERE`.
- Data aggregation functions are often used in combination with the `GROUP BY` clause.
- SQL commands that are used to manage tables are known as DDL. Table management typically involves three commands: `CREATE TABLE`, `ALTER TABLE`, and `DROP TABLE`.
- You can insert a single row or multiple rows of data into a table via the `INSERT TO ... VALUE ...` statement.

Related tables and more SQL | 2

In this chapter

- You learn what related tables are and how to query them.

- You revisit table and data management.

- You explore how to learn more SQL on your own.

(*continued*)

The easiest approach is to use SQLite Online as follows:

1. Clone or download our GitHub repository (https://github.com/Neo-Hao/grokking-relational-database-design).

2. Locate the scripts in the `chapter_02` folder.

3. Visit SQLite Online (https://sqliteonline.com). Choose your target RDBMS in the left sidebar and click Click to Connect.

4. Click Import to load the script corresponding to your chosen RDBMS (such as `mysql_db.sql` from the downloaded or cloned GitHub repository for MariaDB).

5. Click Okay.

Overview

In chapter 1, you learned the basics of SQL, and you learned how to query or create a single table. In this chapter, you will continue learning a bit more of SQL by querying and creating related tables. Then you will peek into how to pick up more SQL keywords by yourself in the future.

Related tables

In this section, you will learn how to work with two or more tables that are related. These *related tables* are tables in a database that are connected by one or more common columns. The Sci-Fi Collective, for example (the online store you know from chapter 1), allows customers to create user accounts, shop online, and leave reviews for the products they bought. The Sci-Fi Collective is supported by a database composed of multiple tables. Among these tables are two that are related: `product` and `review`. The `product` table represents the products that are sold, and the `review` table represents the reviews customers leave for the products they bought. The two tables have a common column (`product_id`). The relationship between the two tables is summarized in the following figure:

The `product_id` column is shared by the `product` and `review` tables. In the `product` table, the `product_id` column is the primary key. In the `review` table, the `product_id` column is known as the *foreign key*, which refers to the primary key of another table. In this case, the other table is `product`.

In other words, the value in the `product_id` column helps connect a row in the `product` table and a row in the `review` table. In the `product` table, for example, the row with a `product_id` value of 3 records a product named Cat-Poop Coffee; in the `review` table, the row with a `review_id` value of 1 records a positive review for Cat-Poop Coffee. How would you know that the review is for Cat-Poop Coffee? The two rows have the same `product_id` value.

Number(s) of shared columns

As curious as you are, you may wonder whether the `product` and `review` tables can share a few more columns. That's a great question about database design. A more generalized question would be whether two related tables should share columns beyond the primary/foreign key(s). The answer is no.

To simplify our discussion, let's look at the scenario in which two related tables use single columns as the primary keys: the `product` and `review` tables. Theoretically speaking, the number of columns shared by two related tables can range from only the primary/foreign key(s) to all columns from both tables. Using the `product` and `review` tables as an example, the following figure summarizes this spectrum:

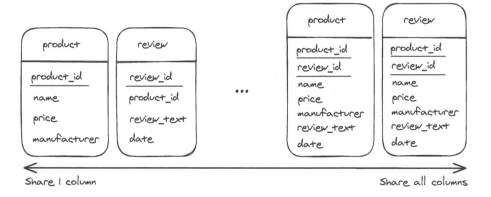

If two related tables share every column, it is obvious that one of them is redundant and thus unnecessary. If you choose to delete one of them, you will find yourself dealing with a problem similar to one you saw in chapter 1: using one table to represent two entities, which will lead to insertion or delete anomalies. OK, making two tables share every column is a bad idea.

How about making the two tables share only a few columns, such as one or two columns beyond the primary/foreign key(s)? That's also a bad idea. First, you would still have redundancy, even if it's less serious than a redundant table. Second, you will set a trap for yourself when you need to update data in such tables. If you update data in only one table and forget the other, you will end up with inconsistent data.

Suppose that you decide to make the `product` and `review` tables share one more column—`manufacturer`—in addition to `product_id`. When you need to update the manufacturer of a product, you have to update both the `product` and `review` tables. Otherwise, you will end up with new manufacturer data in one table but old data in the other. Such a problem is known as an *update anomaly*. As you can see in the following figure, two related tables shouldn't share columns beyond the primary/foreign key(s).

product_id	name	price	manufacturer
1	Atomic Nose ...	19.99	Mad Inventors Inc.
2	Selfie Toaster	24.99	Goofy Gadgets Corp.
3	Cat-Poop Coffee	29.99	Absurd Accessories
...	...	...	...

update to:

Mad Inventors Inc.

conflict with

review_id	product_id	manufacturer	review_text	date
1	3	Absurd Accessories	Great product ...	2023-...
2	5	Silly Supplies Co.	...best thing ...	2023-...
3	2	Goofy Gadgets Corp.	...not recommend	2023-...
...	...	...	...	...

Join data from related tables

From time to time, you will need to join data from related tables. If you want to know about how each product of The Sci-Fi Collective is reviewed, for example, you will need to join at least the product name from the product table and the corresponding product reviews from the review table and then make sure that data from both tables is joined properly. In SQL, you can write the query that does this job as follows:

```
SELECT name, review_text
FROM product
JOIN review
ON product.product_id = review.product_id;
```

This query yields the following result:

name	review_text
Cat-Poop Coffee	Great product ...
Unicorn Horn Polish	This is the best ...
Selfie Toaster	Not worth the money ...
...	...

We need to explain quite a few things about this query:

- What is the general syntax for retrieving data from related tables?
- What does the `JOIN...ON...` clause do?
- What is the dot, and how do we use dot notation as in `product.product_id` and `review.product_id`?

What is the general syntax for retrieving data from related tables? The general syntax is

```
SELECT column1, column2, ...
FROM table1
JOIN table2
ON table1.column = table2.column;
```

What does the `JOIN...ON` clause do? Suppose that you have two toy boxes, one with cars and the other with racetracks. You want to play with both kinds of toys, so you pour all the toys from both boxes onto the floor; then you need to find which cars would work on what types of racetracks. That's what the `JOIN` clause does.

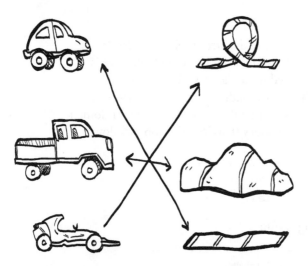

In detail, the `JOIN` clause takes two tables (toy boxes) and pours all the rows (toys) on the floor; then it looks for matching values in the shared column (like the match between a car and a racetrack) between the

two tables. If it finds a match, it puts the corresponding rows (cars and trucks that go together) together in a new table (your play area).

What is the dot, and how do we use dot notation as in `product.product_id` and `review.product_id`? *Dot notation* is SQL syntax used to separate parts of a name. `product.product_id`, for example, refers to the `product_id` column in the `product` table. As another example, `product.name` can refer to the `name` column in the `product` table. Dot notation is especially handy when you query related tables because it helps you to be specific about the columns in case they have the same name, such as `product.product_id` and `review.product_id`. This approach makes it clear which column and which table you are referring to and prevents confusion.

If two tables that you want to join have multiple columns that share a name, you may want to rename them in the SELECT statement to prevent confusion. Otherwise, you might end up with a result set that looks like a mixed-up game of Scrabble played by a mischievous toddler.

Suppose that you have two related tables, `employee` and `department`, and you want to join them to get the names of the departments to which employees belong.

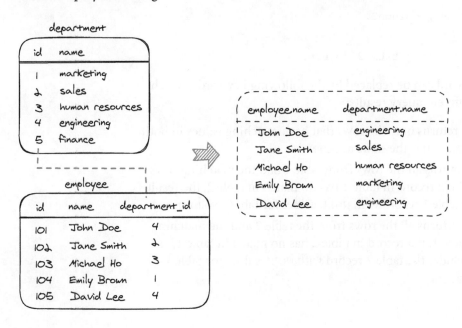

Both tables have a column named `name`, so you need to use dot notation to specify which `name` column to select:

```
SELECT employee.name, department.name
FROM employee
JOIN department
ON employee.department_id = department.id;
```

Depending on the RDBMS you use, you may see the same column names, as in the preceding figure, or two identical column names (such as `name`). To prevent confusion, you can rename the columns with an alias via the `AS` clause:

```
SELECT employees.name AS employee_name,
       departments.name AS department_name
FROM employees
JOIN departments
ON employees.department_id = departments.id;
```

Types of JOINS

Now that you know the basics of the `JOIN` clause, we'll dive a bit deeper into joins by discussing their variations. Before we do so, we'll try to refresh your memory on the general syntax of joining tables:

```
SELECT column1, column2, ...
FROM table1
JOIN table2
ON table1.column = table2.column;
```

The `JOIN` keyword can be replaced by the following keywords, which may lead to different query results:

- `INNER JOIN` returns only the rows that have matching values in both tables; `INNER JOIN` is the same as `JOIN`.
- `LEFT JOIN` returns all the rows from table 1 and the matching rows from table 2. If a record in table 1 has no match in table 2, the result includes the table 1 record with `NULL` values for table 2 columns.
- `RIGHT JOIN` returns all the rows from the table 2 and the matching rows from table 1. If a record in table 2 has no match in table 1, the result includes the table 2 record with `NULL` values for table 1 columns.

- `FULL OUTER JOIN` returns all the rows from both tables, including the nonmatching rows. If a record in table 1 has a matching record in table 2, the result includes a single row with data from both tables. If a record in table 1 has no match in table 2, the result includes the table 1 record with `NULL` values for table 2 columns; if a record in table 2 has no match in table 1, the result includes the table 2 record with `NULL` values for table 1 columns.

The relationships among the left table, the right table, and the returned results are summarized in the following figure:

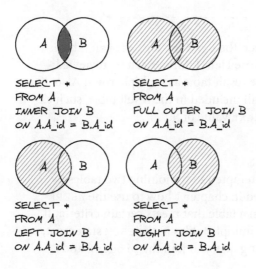

It is worth noting that `LEFT JOIN`, `RIGHT JOIN`, and `FULL OUTER JOIN` may lead to query results with `NULL` values. One side effect of getting `NULL` values in the result is that you need to handle them carefully. `NULL` values can cause errors if you try to perform calculations or comparison. (As an example, 10 + `NULL` will lead to `NULL`.) Our `product` table, for example, contains some new products in our store that have not been reviewed by any users. When we perform a `LEFT JOIN` between the `product` and `review` tables, we end up with some rows that have `NULL` values in the columns from the `review` table. The `LEFT JOIN` query would be

```
SELECT name, review_text
FROM product
LEFT JOIN review
ON product.product_id = review.product_id;
```

This query yields the following result:

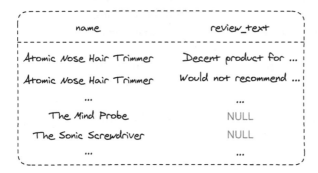

As you can see, every match between the `product` and `review` table is included. A product like Atomic Nose Hair Trimmer can be reviewed more than once and show up in the result table as multiple rows. Also, if a product was not reviewed, it is still included in the result table, such as The Mind Probe, with a `review_text` value of `NULL`.

WHERE vs. JOIN

As curious as you are, you may be tempted to try joining two tables by using the `WHERE` clause. You learned in chapter 1 how to use the `WHERE` clause to filter a subset of data from a table that meets certain criteria. If you know that it is possible to list multiple tables in the `FROM` statement, you might put together the following query to join the `product` and `review` tables you saw earlier:

```
SELECT name, review_text
FROM product, review
WHERE product.product_id = review.product_id;
```

Would this query work and yield the same result as the example we saw earlier? Yes. This query will work fine to join the two tables, and it yields the same result as the query using the `JOIN` clause:

```
SELECT name, review_text
FROM product
JOIN review
ON product.product_id = review.product_id;
```

Whenever you need to query related tables, however, `JOIN` is generally preferred to `WHERE` for at least three reasons:

- *Readability*—Explicit `JOIN` makes the query's intention clearer and easier to understand.
- *Maintainability*—Explicit `JOIN` is less prone to errors and more straightforward to modify or debug.
- *Optimization*—When you use a `WHERE` clause to query two related tables, the query essentially asks for a cross join between the two tables, which is more difficult for most RDBMSs to optimize than an explicit `JOIN`.

Cross join: A wild dance in which everyone twirls with everyone else

A *cross join* in SQL is an operation that combines every row from one table with every row from another table. It generates all possible combinations of rows between the two tables, returning a huge result.

If the `FROM` clause in your query is followed by two or more tables, your query will perform a cross join between those tables. `FROM product, review`, for example, means that every row in the `product` table will be paired with every row in the `review` table whether or not a match exists.

Cross joins may require scanning the involved tables separately, and they demand a large amount of memory from the RDBMS.

Revisit table and data management

This section explores how to manage related tables and their data. In chapter 1, you learned how to manage a single table and its data. In the preceding section, you worked with a pair of related tables that we gave you. Now you will apply what you learned in chapter 1 and the preceding section to expand your knowledge of table and data management to related tables.

Manage related tables

You will learn how to create related tables from the prepared scripts that accompany this chapter. The scripts aim to create two related tables, product and review, for the database supporting The Sci-Fi Collective and to populate them with a set of sample data. You need to pick the script that works with your target RDBMS, of course (such as mysql_db.sql for MySQL or MariaDB).

You create the product table the same way that you did in chapter 1:

```
CREATE TABLE product (
  product_id INT PRIMARY KEY,
  name TEXT NOT NULL,
  description TEXT NOT NULL,
  price DECIMAL(5, 2) NOT NULL,
  manufacturer TEXT NOT NULL
);
```

You create the review table as follows:

```
-- comment: works for MySQL and MariaDB
-- comment: see the code repo for other RDBMS
CREATE TABLE review (
  review_id INT PRIMARY KEY,
  product_id INT NOT NULL,
  review_text TEXT NOT NULL,
  datetime DATETIME NOT NULL
    DEFAULT CURRENT_TIMESTAMP,
  CONSTRAINT fk_product_review
    FOREIGN KEY (product_id)
    REFERENCES product (product_id)
);
```

We need to answer two questions about this query:

- What is the general syntax for creating two tables that have a relationship?
- What does the `CONSTRAINT...FOREIGN KEY...REFERENCES...` clause do?

What is the general syntax for creating two tables that have a relationship? As you know, the shared column `product_id` is the primary key in the `product` table and the foreign key in the `review` table. Given a pair of two related tables, we call a table like `product` the *parent table* because it uses the shared column as the primary key. We call a table like `review` the *child table* because it holds the foreign key.

As you can see from the command that creates the `product` table, the syntax for creating a parent table is the same as the syntax for creating a single table that is not related to other tables.

To create a child table, you need to specify the foreign key that references the primary key in the parent table. You still need to define all the columns, data types, and the primary key, of course. The general syntax for creating a child table is

```
CREATE TABLE child_table_name (
  column1 datatype1 [NOT NULL],
  column2 datatype2 [NOT NULL],
  ...,
  foreign_key_column datatype,
  CONSTRAINT fk_parent_child
    FOREIGN KEY (foreign_key_column) REFERENCES
    parent_table_name(parent_table_primary_key)
);
```

Alternatively, you can create the two tables independently and add the foreign key constraint to the child table afterward:

```
-- comment: assuming the parent and child tables
-- comment: have been created
ALTER TABLE child_table_name
  ADD CONSTRAINT fk_parent_child
    FOREIGN KEY (foreign_key_column) REFERENCES
    parent_table_name(parent_table_primary_key);
```

What does the CONSTRAINT...FOREIGN KEY...REFERENCES... clause do? In short, the clause creates a foreign key constraint, which serves as a link between two related tables. The constraint is twofold:

- The constraint ensures that the foreign key column in the child table references only valid primary key values in the parent table.
- The constraint ensures that the updating or deletion of rows in the parent table doesn't violate the consistency between two related tables.

We refer to these two aspects as *referential integrity*. The CONSTRAINT... FOREIGN KEY...REFERENCES... clause enforces referential integrity between two related tables.

If you take a closer look at the CONSTRAINT...FOREIGN KEY... REFERENCES... clause, you can divide it into two parts, as shown in the following figure.

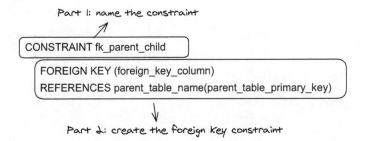

The FOREIGN KEY...REFERENCES... statement creates the foreign key constraint that enforces referential integrity. The CONSTRAINT... clause allows you to name this constraint. When you create a foreign key constraint, you don't necessarily need to name it, but naming it will make it easy to access whenever you need to modify such a constraint in the future. We named the foreign key constraint fk_product_ review in the review table, for example. If we ever need to drop this constraint, we can access the constraint via this name:

```
-- comment: SQLite doesn't support ALTER TABLE
-- comment: DROP CONSTRAINT
ALTER TABLE review
  DROP CONSTRAINT fk_product_review;
```

If you don't name a constraint yourself, the RDBMS will name it automatically, using its default naming convention. Although the automatically-picked name can be retrieved, this name and the default naming convention vary from one RDBMS to another. To avoid this hassle, we recommend that you always name constraints (as you should always name pets). After all, dropping or disabling a constraint can be a common task whenever you need to modify your database design.

Manage data in related tables

The syntax for adding, updating, and deleting data in related tables remains the same as you saw in chapter 1. The scripts that we prepared for this chapter added a set of data to both the product and review tables:

```
-- comment: add data to the product table
INSERT INTO product (product_id, name,
                description, price, manufacturer)
VALUES (
  1,
  'Atomic Nose Hair Trimmer',
  'Trim your nose hairs … an atomic clock!',
```

```
   19.99,
   'Mad Inventors Inc.'
),
...;

-- comment: add data to the review table
INSERT INTO review (review_id, product_id,
              review_text, datetime)
VALUES (
   1,
   3,
   'Great product, would definitely recommend!',
   '2022-01-01 12:30:00'
),
...;
```

What makes data management for related tables different, however, is the foreign key constraint. Earlier in this chapter, you learned that the foreign key constraint enforces referential integrity on a pair of two related tables:

- The foreign key constraint ensures that the foreign key column in the child table references only valid primary key values in the parent table.
- The foreign key constraint ensures that the deletion of rows in the parent table doesn't violate the consistency between two related tables.

When you try to add data to the child table, the new data needs to be consistent with the existing data in the parent table; otherwise, the RDBMS will complain. Suppose that you are trying to add a new row of review data to the review table, but the product_id value (such as 3000) in this row can't be found in the product table:

```
INSERT INTO review (review_id, product_id,
              review_text, datetime)
VALUES (
   1,
   3000,
   'Great product!',
   '2023-05-01 12:30:00'
);
```

When you execute this command, your RDBMS will give you an error message similar to the following:

```
ERROR 1452 (23000):
Cannot add or update a child row:
a foreign key constraint fails …
```

Likewise, when you alter or delete data from the parent table, the alteration or deletion shouldn't lead to orphan data records in the child table; if it does, the RDBMS will complain. Suppose that you want to delete a row of product data from the `product` table, but this product data is referenced in the `review` table. If you delete this row, the deletion will create some orphan review data in the `review` table. Fortunately, the foreign key constraint will stop this situation from happening, and you will get an error message similar to the following:

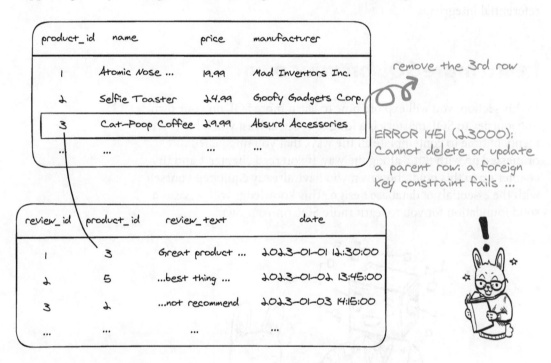

remove the 3rd row

ERROR 1451 (23000):
Cannot delete or update
a parent row: a foreign
key constraint fails ...

The ultimate form of deleting data records from the parent table is dropping the table entirely. If this action is ever allowed, all the data in the child table will become orphan data. Fortunately, the foreign key constraint stops it from happening, and you get an error message similar to the following:

```
ERROR: cannot drop table … because other objects depend
on it
DETAIL: constraint… on table…depends on table…
```

If you are still in the process of perfecting your database design and need to modify the table structure, you can refer to chapter 1 to see how to modify an individual table, or see the preceding section to find out how to alter the foreign key constraint. In an extreme scenario, you may need to drop a pair of related tables with some sample data. In this case, always save the data first, and drop the child table before dropping the parent table. This order is important because dropping the child table first also eliminates the foreign key constraint. Otherwise, you will see the error message in the preceding figure because the foreign key constraint works hard to enforce the referential integrity.

Learn more SQL on your own

In this section, you will explore how to learn more SQL on your own. The journey to SQL mastery is a long one, but at least you'll have plenty of time to contemplate all the ways that you misspelled SELECT or messed up with NULL along the way. If you read chapter 1 and this chapter up to this point, however, you have already equipped yourself with the essentials of database design. This knowledge will serve as a solid foundation for you to learn more SQL on your own.

In this brave new age, mastering SQL on your own is significantly easier than it was a few years ago due to the rise of generative AI tools such as ChatGPT and Google Gemini. Please make no mistake: we are not advocating relying on ChatGPT solely for learning SQL. If you use generative AI tools like ChatGPT well, you will be able to gain new knowledge quickly and efficiently, and we want to demonstrate how you can use these tools to facilitate learning SQL.

Some aspects of learning SQL remain the same as in the past, of course. You need help from a quality book to learn SQL systematically, especially conceptual knowledge such as indexing and query order of execution. This step can't be replaced by asking ChatGPT questions. Many quality SQL books are available, including these two examples:

- *Learn SQL in a Month of Lunches*, by Jeff Iannucci (https://www.manning.com/books/learn-sql-in-a-month-of-lunches)
- *Learning SQL*, 3rd ed., by Alan Beaulieu (https://mng.bz/Ge5V)

Some other aspects of learning SQL can be very different and more efficient nowadays, especially when you have questions or want to know how a SQL keyword is used. The greatest advantage of generative AI tools such as ChatGPT is that they can provide relatively reliable just-in-time help on common questions. Without such tools, you need to go through an iterative process to get your questions answered, which involves creating a search query, searching online, and filtering the returned search results. This process—especially filtering all the search results—can be daunting.

The wide availability of generative AI tools can help you avoid this iterative process. If you want to know how to use the `sum` aggregate function, for example, you can ask ChatGPT the following question:

> Question: How do I use the sum aggregate function in SQL?

The answer is typically composed of the general syntax and a concrete example, which is as good as and sometimes better than some tutorials written by human beings.

A sample answer from ChatGPT is as follows:

Chatgpt

In Sql, The `Sum` Function Is Used To Calculate The Total Of A Set Of Values In A Column Of A Table. Here's The Basic Syntax:

```
Select Sum(Column_name) From Table_name;
```

For Example, Let's Say We Have A Table Called Orders With The Following Columns: `Id`, `Customer_name`, `Product_name`, And `Price`. If We Wanted To Calculate The Total Revenue From All Orders, We Could Use The Following Query:

```
Select Sum(Price) From Orders;
```

This Would Return A Single Value Representing The Total Sum Of All Prices In The Price Column Of The Orders Table.

If you still find the answer difficult to chew, you can ask ChatGPT to be more patient and explain in detail:

Question: How do I use the sum aggregate function in SQL? Explain with more examples and as if I am five.

You will find that ChatGPT answers this question better than most tutors can. A sample answer from ChatGPT follows:

ChatGPT

Sure! Let's say you have a table with some numbers in it, like this:

```
+----+-------+
| ID | Value |
+----+-------+
|  1 |     2 |
|  2 |     4 |
|  3 |     6 |
|  4 |     8 |
+----+-------+
```

Each row has a number in the Value column. You can think of these numbers like pieces of candy. The ID column is like a label that helps us tell the difference between the pieces of candy.

Now, let's say you want to know how many pieces of candy you have in total. You could count each piece of candy one by one, but that would take a long time. Instead, you can use the SUM function in SQL to add up all the pieces of candy for you! Here's what the SQL query would look like:

```
SELECT SUM(Value) FROM my_table;
```

When you run this query, the computer will add up all the numbers in the Value column for you. In this case, the total is 20. You can think of this as having 20 pieces of candy in total! Here's another example. Let's say you have a table with some prices in it, like this:

```
+----+-------+
| ID | Price |
+----+-------+
|  1 |  1.99 |
|  2 |  2.99 |
|  3 |  3.99 |
|  4 |  4.99 |
+----+-------+
```

Each row has a price in the Price column. You can think of these prices like the cost of buying things, like toys or candy. If you want to know how much money you would need to buy all these things, you can use the SUM function in SQL. Here's what the query would look like:

```
SELECT SUM(Price) FROM my_table;
```

When you run this query, the computer will add up all the prices in the Price column for you. In this case, the total is 13.96. You can think of this as how much money you would need to buy all these things!

One of the most significant benefits of generative AI tools in SQL learning is that they can provide relatively reliable just-in-time help. For common questions, you don't necessarily need to ask the perfect question to receive immediate answers that are informative and well-structured. What's more, in contrast to fine-tuning search engine queries, it's easier to tune your questions to get better answers.

Recap

- Related tables are tables in a database that are connected by a common column.
- In general, it is a bad idea to have related tables share columns beyond the primary/foreign key(s).
- The general syntax for querying two related tables is

```
SELECT column1, column2, ...
FROM table1
JOIN table2
ON table1.column = table2.column;
```

- The most common join types include INNER JOIN, LEFT JOIN, RIGHT JOIN, and OUTER JOIN. INNER JOIN is the same as JOIN, returning only the rows that have matching values in two tables. The other three types may return nonmatching values from one or two tables.
- In general, the JOIN clause is preferred to the WHERE clause for querying related tables.
- Given a pair of two related tables, the table that uses the shared column(s) as the primary key(s) is typically known as the parent table. The table that holds the foreign key(s) is typically known as the child table.
- You can create the parent table the same way that you create a table that is not related to other tables.
- The general syntax for creating a child table is

```
CREATE TABLE child_table_name (
  column1 datatype1 [NOT NULL],
  column2 datatype2 [NOT NULL],
  ...,
  foreign_key_column datatype,
  CONSTRAINT fk_parent_child
    FOREIGN KEY (foreign_key_column)
    REFERENCES
            parent_table_name(
                parent_table_primary_key
            )
);
```

- The foreign key constraint enforces referential integrity in related tables. Referential integrity applies to both table and data management in related tables.
- In general, it is a good idea to name the foreign key constraint when creating related tables.
- Taking advantage of generative AI tools like ChatGPT can make learning SQL more efficient.

In this chapter

- You learn about the goals of database design.

- You get an overview of the database design process.

- You jump-start the requirement analysis.

What you need to know

This chapter provides an overview of database design from a bird's-eye view. That said, this chapter doesn't have accompanying scripts like those in chapters 1 and 2.

Overview

In chapters 1 and 2, you learned the basics of relational databases and SQL. Starting with this chapter, you will embark on your journey of learning database design by designing a database from scratch for the online store of The Sci-Fi Collective. In this chapter, you will get an overview of the goals and process of database design. After that, you will jump-start the requirement analysis for The Sci-Fi Collective.

Goals of database design

The overall goal of database design is to deliver a well-structured, efficient database that meets the requirements of users and organizations. Beyond meeting these requirements, a successful database design typically meets five common goals:

- Data consistency and integrity
- Maintainability and ease of use
- Performance and optimization
- Data security
- Scalability and flexibility

In this section, you will peek at these goals to better understand what you should aim to achieve in database design.

Data consistency and integrity

Data consistency and integrity are about defining appropriate data types, constraints, and relationships among entities to ensure that

- Data remains consistent across tables.
- Data redundancy is minimized.
- Anomalies are prevented.

In chapters 1 and 2, you peeked at some poor designs that led to data redundancy and learned about three types of anomalies. In short, data consistency means taking measures to ensure that those problems don't happen.

Insertion, update, and delete anomalies

An *insertion anomaly* occurs when adding a new record to a database requires adding unrelated data.

An *update anomaly* happens when modifying data results in inconsistencies within the data.

A *delete anomaly* happens when removing data leads to unintentional loss of information.

Maintainability and ease of use

A well-designed database should be intuitive to use and easy to maintain by the people who use it, including database administrators, data analysts, and developers of web or mobile applications that are powered by the database.

You can take a lot of measures to increase the maintainability and ease of use of a database. Following a consistent naming convention, for example, is a small thing to do when you design a database, but it can save a lot of time for people who use or maintain the database. If developers who use a database have to spend time figuring out whether and where `id`, `Id`, and `identifier` are used as the primary key columns, the database is hardly intuitive to use, let alone easy to maintain. Think about having to maintain a database with the following tables:

INCONSISTENT USE OF IDs

PRODUCT

(Product_id)
name
price
manufacturer

REVIEW

(reviewId)
product_id
review_text
date

USER

(user_identifier)
username
email
password

PAYMENT

(paymentKey)
cardNumber
esc
expiryDate

Performance and optimization

A well-designed database should optimize query performance and reduce response time. An efficient database can help save running costs and boost the performance of the applications it supports, which in turn will enhance the user experience.

You can take a lot of measures to optimize the performance of a database. The data in the `review` table you saw in chapter 2, for example, often needs to be sorted because the table and its database support the online store of The Sci-Fi Collective, and potential customers often want to see the latest reviews of the products they browse. You can index the date column in the `review` table to speed the sorting operation.

What is indexing? Think of the data in the review table as being a library of books. *Indexing* is the process of creating an index-card catalog that lists every book alphabetically along with its location. When you need to sort, you can use the index-card catalog to locate every book and put it in its sorted position.

Remember card catalogs?

Data security

A well-designed database should have robust security measures in place. In other words, a well-designed database prevents unauthorized access, insertion, modification, or deletion. Even when such problems happen, the sensitive data should still be well protected and easy to recover.

You can take a lot of measures to safeguard the data. If you ever need to store payment method information in your database, for example, you should store only encrypted information. Storing customers' payment method information in plain text is a bad idea. If an evil hacker gains access to the database, they will know everyone's credit card number. By contrast, encryption helps protect sensitive information even in a worst-case scenario.

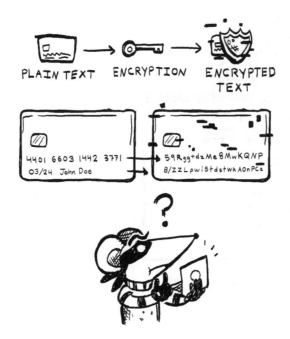

Scalability and flexibility

A well-designed and efficient database should accommodate growth and changing requirements without sacrificing performance (trying to have your cake and eat it too).

You can take various measures to enhance the scalability and flexibility of your database design. When you design your database schema, for example, separating tables can make them smaller, which in turn can speed data lookups. Also, you can implement a cache mechanism for frequently accessed data, such as the product information in The Sci-Fi Collective's database. *Caching* involves storing frequently accessed data in fast-access memory, such as RAM, which can significantly improve database performance and responsiveness, particularly as the data size grows. Popular caching systems such as Redis (https://redis.io) and Memcached (https://www.memcached.org) can implement this mechanism.

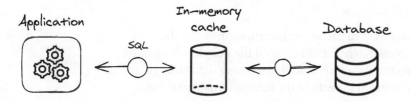

Overview of the design process

In this section, we review the overall database design process by covering the key phases and steps in database design. Some approaches to database design emphasize a well-defined sequential process such as the waterfall approach, in which each phase must be completed before moving to the next. Other approaches, such as the agile approach, focus on an iterative, and flexible approach, allowing for adjustments as the project unfolds. Despite the differences, all database design approaches have the same key phases:

- Requirement gathering
- Analysis and design
- Implementation/integration and testing

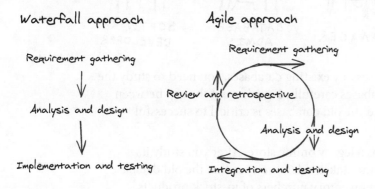

Requirement gathering

Requirement gathering refers to gathering information about the database in different ways, such as talking to all the people who will be involved with or using the database, studying existing databases (if any), and examining other relevant aspects of information management.

To talk to all the people who will be involved with or using the database, you need to organize meetings, ask good questions, and have conversations with different groups. To build the database for The Sci-Fi Collective, you would talk to shop owners and managers, future database administrators, and software developers who will build the web and mobile applications to find out what kind of information they need to keep track of.

If a legacy application uses any existing databases, you need to study the application and the databases carefully. Figuring out the gap between current expectations and the old databases is critical to successful database design.

The Sci-Fi Collective has a legacy online store. After you study its database and talk to all the stakeholders, you see that the old database doesn't support tracking inventory numbers of in-stock products, which sometimes leads to customers buying products that are no longer in stock. The developers of The Sci-Fi Collective's web app want the new database to track inventory numbers so that the web app can let customers know promptly when a particular product goes out of stock.

Any information management within the organization that is expected to be part of the database you design is also relevant. The purchasing manager of The Sci-Fi Collective used to manage the inventory information by using a spreadsheet and a paper form. To make such management activities part of your database design, you need to study the paper form, the spreadsheet, and the management flow.

Analysis and design

The analysis and design phase involves carefully thinking through all the requirements and coming up with a solid plan for how the database will be structured and how it will work. In the end, you will create a detailed blueprint of the database. Some key steps in this phase include data modeling and normalization.

Data modeling aims to create a conceptual design that shows how the parts of a database fit together and relate to one another. The conceptual design is typically represented visually as an entity-relationship (E-R) diagram. An E-R diagram for the database of The Sci-Fi Collective might look like this:

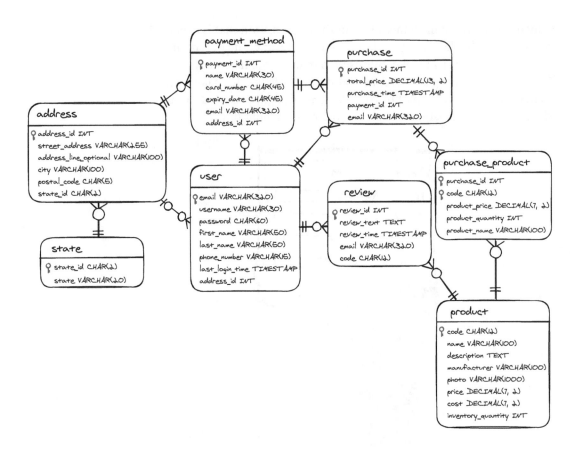

We know that this diagram contains symbols and syntax that you may not understand yet. You will learn about them, as well as learn how to model data using E-R diagrams, in chapter 5.

Normalization comes after the E-R diagram is established. Normalization minimizes redundancy by breaking down a table representing more than one entity into smaller, logical units and organizing them in separate tables. As an example, someone designed a `product_review` table to hold data on both products and their reviews. As you saw in chapter 2, storing information about more than one entity in the same table can lead to redundancy and anomalies. You could normalize such a table by breaking it into two tables: `product` and `review`.

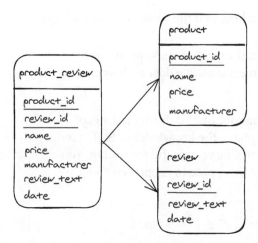

You will learn more about normalization and see how to determine whether a table needs to be normalized in chapter 6.

Implementation/integration and testing

The implementation/integration and testing phase involves building and validating the database based on the blueprint you made in the design and analysis phase. If you use the waterfall approach, the database is implemented all at the same time; if you use the agile approach, the database is implemented part by part and integrated into what has been implemented. Then you test the database to ensure that it functions correctly, performs well, and meets the intended requirements.

During implementation, you create the tables, define the columns and their data types, establish relationships between tables, apply any constraints or rules specified in your design blueprint, and determine which columns to index to optimize query performance. You learned how to use SQL to create a single table or related tables in chapters 1 and 2, and that knowledge can be very useful for this step.

After the database has been implemented, you want to test it before putting it to use. Typically, testing a database needs to validate at least three aspects:

- *Functionality*—You need to check whether the database performs the expected tasks correctly, such as creating, updating, and deleting a data entry.

- *Performance*—You need to check how well the database handles large amounts of data or heavy use.
- *Security*—You need to verify that the database has appropriate security measures in place to protect sensitive data such as passwords and payment methods.

You should identify and fix any bugs discovered during testing, of course. As in the implementation phase, the knowledge of SQL queries you gained from chapters 1 and 2 will be very useful for testing. You will learn more about the details of this phase in chapters 6 and 7.

Key phases of database design

In the preceding section, you got an overview of the process of database design. Starting with this section, you will explore and learn the key phases in database design by designing a database for the online store of The Sci-Fi Collective from scratch. Working on a project from scratch will give you hands-on experience and detailed knowledge of components you would otherwise not pick up.

In this section, you will learn more about the first key phase in database design: requirement gathering. Because requirement gathering is an art rather than a science, following the advice and insights of experts and veterans in this trade can make your life much easier.

The goals of the database

As you take on requirement-gathering tasks, you need to answer a critical question based on all the information to collect: what are the goals of the database?

Every database is created for some specific purpose, whether that purpose is to handle the daily transactions of a business or manage the information of an organization. You need to identify the goal of the database clearly because the database will be used to make important decisions.

Sometimes, it takes longer than expected to come to a full understanding of the goals of the database, and you need to be ready for that situation. To have a good understanding of the goal of the database for The Sci-Fi Collective, you need to interview the owner, managers, staff, and software developers. You can summarize the goals of this database as follows:

> The database of The Sci-Fi Collective is to maintain information about products, such as their inventory and reviews, and information about users, such as their payment information and purchases, as well as the transaction information linking users and products.

Existing databases and other aspects of information management

Sometimes you can refer to an existing database for your work. If so, you should resist the urge to base your new design on the structure of the existing database. There is a good reason why the organization/business decided to hire you to design a database from scratch instead of modifying the old database. Although the existing database can contain valuable information in terms of what entities and attributes are required to structure some tables, you must be careful about potential design errors in the existing database. Also, you must recognize that it will take the same amount of effort to figure out the demands of the new database and how they differ from those of the existing database.

How do you figure out the current demands? Conduct interviews. How do you figure out the gap between the existing database and current demands? Conduct more interviews with more questions.

With respect to other aspects of information management, you may find that many people discovered ingenious ways to use word processors, spreadsheets, and paper forms to collect and manage data effectively. If this type of data management needs to be part of the new database you're designing, you may want to do at least two things:

- *Get a subject-matter expert (SME) to walk you through how the data is managed.* This walk-through should involve demonstration and stepwise explanation because it is usually difficult to grasp data management through interviews alone.
- *Ask for data samples whenever possible.* The data samples will play an important role in helping you verify the attributes and data types in the next phase of database design.

We'll use an example to illustrate the preceding two points. The purchasing manager of The Sci-Fi Collective currently manages all the inventory data in a spreadsheet, and the database you design will eventually replace the spreadsheet to manage that data. Instead of talking only to this manager and the purchasing team, you want them to walk you through the whole process of purchasing a batch of products, such as ordering, entering data about a new product, and updating and removing records of products that are already in inventory. The process can be complicated, so getting a demonstration is the best approach whenever possible. More important, you should ask for a copy of the authentic data, which ideally should be anonymized. The data will help clarify many problems that the demonstration can't, such as the exact number of attributes and data types.

	A	B	C	D	F	G
1	Product name	Manufacturer	Description	Cost	Quantities	MSRP
2	Neuro-Enhancer	CyberDyne Corp	Neural implant ...	$499.99	10	$799.99
3	Quantum Flux...	HyperTech Labs	Revolutionary	$999.99	2	$1,999.99
4	Plasma Blaster	NovaArmory	Portable hand ...	$299.99	15	$599.99
5	Nanotech Gel	BioSolutions Inc	Advanced nano...	$79.99	50	$149.99
...	...	...	...	...	...	...

Interviews

Interviews are the most important tasks in requirement gathering. During and after the interviews, you need to identify three pieces of information: subjects, characteristics, and relationships among subjects. These three pieces of information will be critical to helping you sail through the next phase of database design.

Relationships are self-explanatory, but what are subjects and characteristics? *Subjects* are people, places, things, events, and the like. *Characteristics* are the features of subjects.

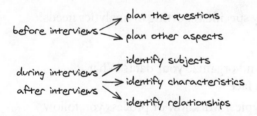

Prepare for interviews

Before conducting interviews, carefully plan the questions and other aspects of the interviews. What questions should you prepare? The answer depends on the project as well as whom you are interviewing. To simplify the problem, you may want to group the people you interview. Although the number of groups can vary, a business or organization typically has at least three groups of people you should consider interviewing: stakeholders, SMEs, and IT/technical staff.

The Sci-Fi Collective happens to be a typical business. It has two owners and one manager, two minotaurs who are responsible for tasks such as data entry and customer service, and three elves who work as software developers. Following are some sample interview questions for each group:

- *Stakeholders*

  What is the primary purpose of the database, and what specific goals do you want to achieve with it?

  What key features or functionalities do you expect the database to support?

  Should the database support any specific reporting or analytics needs?

- *SMEs*

  How do you currently manage and organize your data? What challenges or limitations do you face?

  Can you walk me through the typical workflow or process you follow when working with data?

  What specific information or data elements are most critical to your work?

- *IT/technical staff*

  What are the main tasks or activities you perform that involve data storage or retrieval?

  What reports or outputs do you typically generate from the data? What information do these reports provide?

  Do you perform any specific calculations or computations on the data?

You should prepare more questions for each group yourself. What is the guiding principle for preparing interview questions? A good question should help you gather relevant information about what data the database should store, how the data should be stored, and what constraints should be put in place. If there's no time constraint, however, a bad question is better than no question. If you are new to this process, you can ask for some example questions from ChatGPT. You might ask ChatGPT to provide some sample questions by using a prompt like the following.

> When you need to design a database, you need to conduct interviews with stakeholders. What questions are typically asked during such interviews?

Beyond interview questions, you need to prepare many things beforehand. Here are some key questions that you need to ask yourself during preparation:

- How do you want to record the interview? Will you take notes or record the conversation? If you decide to record, do you need to gain permission from the organization?
- Where do you want to conduct the interviews?
- Do you need to invite more than one group to the same interview? If so, who had better *not* be invited to the same interview? Should there be a limit on the number of interviewees?

Also, ask yourself more questions specific to the project and participants of the interviews. The guiding principle of any preparation is to make the interviews productive and informative.

Identify subjects, characteristics, and relationships

During and after the interviews, you need to identify subjects, characteristics, and relationships among subjects. In case you wonder why, one of the tasks you will take on during the next design phase is mapping the subjects, characteristics, and relationships to entities, attributes, and relationships among entities.

To identify subjects and characteristics during the interview or from the record of the interview, you can look for nouns in the responses to your questions. How do you differentiate subjects from characteristics?

Typically, if you can build a sentence with two nouns in which one *has* or *owns* the other, the one that is possessed is the characteristic, and the other is the subject. You can put *user* and *password* in the following sentence, for example:

A user has a password.

The password is possessed by the user, so it is a characteristic of a user, whereas the user is a subject.

You need to perform similar deductions on interview conversations. You might ask the following question of an IT staff member working for The Sci-Fi Collective:

Q: What are the main tasks or activities you perform that involve data storage or retrieval?

The participant may give you a response like this (in which all subjects that can be identified are underlined):

A: As a software developer, I am mainly responsible for building and maintaining the transaction system of the online store. When a <u>user</u> makes an <u>order</u>, the transaction system is supposed to retrieve the <u>user</u>'s <u>account</u> and <u>payment method</u>, generate an order with all the information for the ordered <u>products</u>, calculate the <u>total price</u>, bill the <u>payment method</u>, and generate an <u>invoice</u>.

This response is very good. The participant answered your question well, with a lot of useful details. You can track all the nouns and see whether they can be used in sentences with the verb *has* or *owns* to identify the subjects and characteristics:

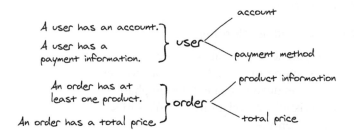

As you can see, it is easy to deduce at least two subjects—user and order—in this response. A user has two characteristics: account and payment method. An order has two characteristics: product information and total price. Two other subjects—invoice and product—don't have any characteristics.

Typically, you need to ask follow-up questions to get all the characteristics of a given subject. You might have this follow-up conversation with a participant:

> Q: What information does a complete order have?
> A: Well, the same as any other online store: the prices and quantities of all the products bought by a customer. That's it. An order is not complicated.
>
> Q: What about the total price? Is the total price a part of the order?
> A: Sort of. Yes. The total price is calculated based on the unit price and quantities of all the bought products.
>
> Q: What about the date and time when an order was put into the system? Is that a necessary piece of information for an order?
> A: Yes, yes. That's absolutely a necessary piece.

Answers such as "the same as any other online store" and "Sort of" are vague, often requiring you to follow up and ask clarification questions. Luckily, the participant provided enough details after such vague answers. Based on the answers, you can update the characteristics of the order subject as follows:

To wrap up the discussion of subjects and characteristics, you should always ask for sample data if possible. When you have a good understanding of the subjects and characteristics discussed by the participant, you could follow up with a question like this:

Q: Can you provide some sample data for products, orders, invoices, and users? Anything will help.

After identifying the subjects and characteristics, you will be ready to ask about relationships among subjects. Your focus should be the relationship between every two subjects. You could ask a follow-up question about the relationship between users and orders:

Q: How are orders related to users? Can a user make multiple orders? Can multiple users contribute to one order?

The participant might give you this response:

A: A user can of course make as many orders as they like. However, our system doesn't support multiple users contributing to one order.

You could ask a follow-up question about the relationship between products and orders:

Q: How are orders related to products? Can an order have more than one product? Can a product show up in more than one order?

The participant might give you a response like this:

A: An order can have more than one product. Vice versa, a product can show up in different orders.

You don't necessarily need to do any analysis of these responses; just record them well.

So far, you have walked through all the necessary steps in an interview. When you finish interviewing all the groups in The Sci-Fi Collective, you will be able to identify a set of subjects and characteristics associated with each subject, as shown in the following figure.

```
user                product              payment method
* username          * code               * name
* email             * name               * credit card number
* password          * description        * expiry date
* first name        * manufacturer       * billing address
* last name         * photo
* phone number      * price
* address           * cost               order
                    * inventory quantity * total price
review                                   * product price
* review text                            * product quantity
* date and time                          * date and time
```

You will also be able to identify the following relationships:

- A user can make multiple orders. An order can be made by only one user.
- A user can review multiple products as long as the user bought those products. A product can be reviewed by multiple users.
- A user can maintain multiple payment methods. A payment method can be associated with only one user.
- An order can have more than one product. A product can show up in multiple orders.

With this information, you are ready to start the next phase in your journey of designing a database for The Sci-Fi Collective.

Recap

- The overall goal of database design is to deliver a well-structured and efficient database.
- Key subgoals of database design include data consistency and integrity, maintainability and ease of use, performance and optimization, data security, and scalability and flexibility.
- All database design approaches have the same key phases, including requirement gathering, analysis and design, and implementation/integration and testing.

- Requirement gathering is the phase in which you gather information about the database in different ways, such as talking to all the people involved in using the database, studying existing databases, and examining other relevant aspects of information management.
- The analysis and design phase focuses on thoroughly understanding all requirements and creating a well-defined plan for the database's structure and functionality.
- The implementation/integration and testing phase is about building and validating the database based on the blueprint you made in the design and analysis phase.
- Conducting interviews is the most important task in requirement gathering. Before interviews, plan the interview questions carefully. During and after the interviews, identify subjects, characteristics, and relationships among subjects.

Part 2
Master database design

Welcome to the heart of database design! This part takes you beyond the basics and into the art and science of creating robust, efficient, and scalable databases. Here, you'll learn how to structure data not just to store it but also to enable powerful, reliable applications.

Chapter 4 begins with entities and attributes—the building blocks of any database. You'll discover how to map real-world objects and concepts to entities and attributes and how to select the right data types.

Chapter 5 focuses on relationships, demonstrating how to create meaningful connections among entities. By the end of this chapter, you'll know how to translate real-world relationships into a coherent, well-structured database.

Chapter 6 introduces normalization and implementation. You'll learn how to refine and strengthen your database designs through normalization and how to translate your designs to SQL, bridging the gap between theory and practice.

Chapter 7 delves into security and optimization. This chapter equips you with strategies to safeguard sensitive data and enhance database performance with techniques such as indexing and denormalization.

By the end of this part, you'll have the expertise to design databases that meet the demands of real-world applications. Whether you're building a small project or tackling a complex enterprise system, this section will prepare you to handle the challenges of modern database design with confidence and precision.

Entities and attributes | 4

• •

In this chapter

- You start the design and analysis phase of database design.

- You learn about keys and common data types in databases.

- You design your first few entities, identifying their attributes, primary keys, and data types.

• •

What you need to know

You can find the database design covered in this chapter (so far, only entities and attributes) implemented in tools commonly used by practitioners, such as dbdiagram.io and MySQL Workbench, in the GitHub repository (https://github.com/Neo-Hao/grokking-relational-database-design). You can navigate to the `chapter_04` folder and follow the instructions in `README.md` to load the database design into corresponding tools.

The data types covered in this chapter apply to most relational database management systems (RDBMSs), such as MySQL, MariaDB, and PostgreSQL. If you use another RDBMS, such as SQL Server or SQLite, you need to make small modifications to the design by replacing certain data types with equivalents specific to the target RDBMS. You can find such information in `README.md` in the `chapter_04` folder.

Overview

In chapter 3, you walked through the database design process and went over the requirements-gathering phase for the online store of The Sci-Fi Collective.

Starting with this chapter, you will move to the next phase of database design: design and analysis. The first step of design and analysis is data modeling, which aims to generate an entity-relationship (E-R) diagram. In this chapter, you will focus on designing all the required entities for the database of The Sci-Fi Collective. By doing so, you will learn about entities, attributes, keys, and data types.

Entities and attributes

In this section, you will focus on turning the subjects and characteristics you deduced from requirements gathering into entities and attributes. The following figure shows the subjects and characteristics for The Sci-Fi Collective:

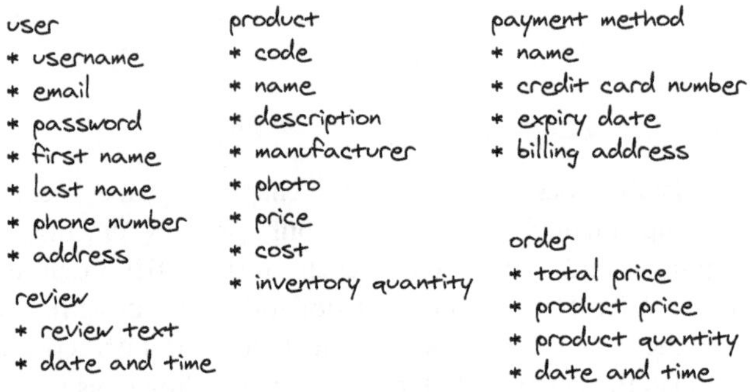

user
* username
* email
* password
* first name
* last name
* phone number
* address

review
* review text
* date and time

product
* code
* name
* description
* manufacturer
* photo
* price
* cost
* inventory quantity

payment method
* name
* credit card number
* expiry date
* billing address

order
* total price
* product price
* product quantity
* date and time

Chapter 1 introduced entities and attributes. Now is a good time to refresh your memory of those concepts. An *entity* is a distinct object or concept that can be described by many attributes. A subject and its characteristics may seem ready to be turned into an entity with attributes with few to no changes. A *subject* is simply an entity, and a *characteristic* is simply an attribute. But you need to put a little bit of thought into naming entities and attributes.

First, you need to choose between singular and plural names for your entities and attributes.

Singular vs. plural: To s or not to s?

Edgar Codd at IBM developed the first RDBMS in the 1970s. In his database, he used singular names for entities (such as `employee`). Other developers followed his lead.

Singular names are best used with primary entities (such as a single `employee` table). Singular approaches have their root in object-oriented programming (OOP), in which a class translates as an entity that contains several objects of the same class.

On the other hand, plural names are more natural as table titles. An `employees` table contains records of employees, for example. Plural table names, however, might cause confusion and errors for someone who isn't sure whether to use plurals in writing queries. Our best recommendation is to aim for consistent use of either convention.

Second, you need to pick a naming convention for the attributes and stick to it. Sticking to a consistent naming convention can prevent typos and other errors in query writing and database maintenance. In this book, we will follow the singular naming convention.

Common naming conventions include

- Snake case (`first_name`)
- Camel case (`firstName`)
- Pascal case (`FirstName`)
- Uppercase (`FIRST_NAME`)
- Hungarian notation, a special case that includes the data type (often abbreviated) as part of the name (`strFirstName`)
- Semantic naming, a special case that includes the purpose of a variable as part of the name (`customerName`)

Among these naming conventions, snake and camel cases are equally popular, followed by Pascal case. Make your choice based on preference and unique software requirements. In this book, we will stick to snake case.

With these two naming decisions made, you can easily map subjects/characteristics to entities/attributes. The `user` subject and its characteristics, for example, can be mapped to the `user` entity and its attributes:

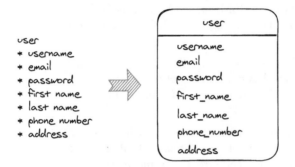

Following the two naming conventions, we will convert all the subjects/characteristics for the online store of The Sci-Fi Collective to the following entities/attributes:

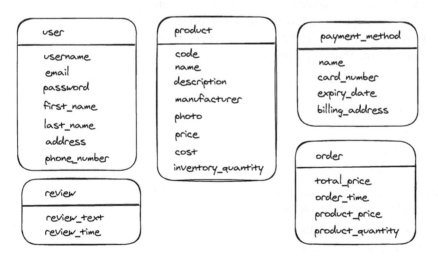

Beyond the naming conventions, you need to check two things about column names:

- *Whether you have names longer than the upper limit*—Many RDBMSs have limits on column-name lengths. MariaDB, for example, limits column names to 64 characters. If you have such a column name, you should shorten it.
- *Whether you used reserved SQL keywords as entity or attribute names*—Using reserved SQL keywords as names can lead to many problems, such as syntax errors in SQL query execution and maintainability problems.

If you use `SELECT` to name an entity, for example, the database system may not understand whether you are referring to the keyword `SELECT` or the entity with that name. Therefore, if you used any reserved keywords as names, you should replace them.

The reserved SQL keywords may vary from one database system to another. You can find a list of keywords in the MySQL documentation (https://mng.bz/zZ6r).

All database systems have a set of common keywords, such as `SELECT`, `ORDER`, `INSERT`, `GROUP`, and `JOIN`. We used the reserved SQL keyword `ORDER` to name one of our entities, so we need to replace it with a different word that has a similar meaning, such as `purchase`:

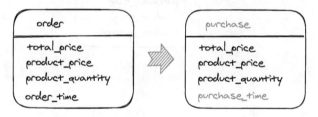

Reserved keywords in SQL

Reserved keywords in SQL have specific meanings and functions. They define, manipulate, and control the database structure and data. The list of reserved keywords can vary depending on the RDBMS, but the most common keywords are used in all RDBMSs.

If you want to know the common reserved keywords, the fastest approach probably is to ask a generative AI tool such as ChatGPT:

(*continued*)

- What are the common reserved keywords in SQL?

If you need to know the reserved keywords of a specific RDBMS, asking a generative AI tool can still be a good start. To find the reserved keywords in MySQL, you can ask ChatGPT the following questions:

- What are the reserved keywords in MySQL?

- Where are the reserved keywords of MySQL listed in its manual?

When you finish all the preceding steps, the entities of The Sci-Fi Collective's online store will look like the following figure:

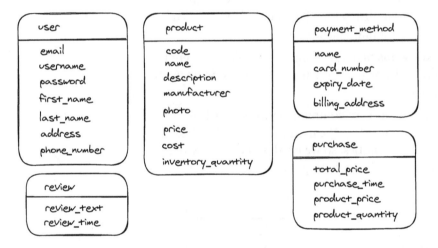

Keys

Now that you have converted the subjects and characteristics you deduced in chapter 2 to entities and attributes, you are ready to start identifying primary keys in each entity.

In chapter 1, you learned about primary keys. A *primary key* refers to one or more attributes that can be used to identify an individual data record. The values of primary keys are unique. A table can have only one primary key.

Why does an entity need a primary key? An entity (set) will eventually be converted to a table in a database. The primary key identifies each row in a table uniquely, enforces data integrity by preventing duplication, and establishes relationships between tables in a relational database. All in all, identifying primary keys is an important step in completing your database design.

The guiding principle in identifying a primary key is simple: pick the best *candidate key* as the primary key. If no good candidate key is available, create a new attribute to serve as the primary key. In this section, we explain what candidate keys are and demonstrate this principle in two examples, starting with the `user` entity.

The `user` entity contains seven attributes. When you put the gathered requirements and sample data side by side, you can easily spot the attributes that should have unique values, preventing duplication of user data:

- `username`—Two users can't have the same username. A new user can't register with a username that's already in the database.
- `email`—Emails must be unique for verification and account recovery. An email address can't be used to register two different users.
- `phone_number`—Phone numbers must be unique for verification and account recovery. Different users can't register the same phone number.

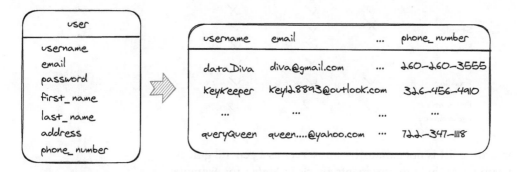

First things first. What is a candidate key? The three attributes are three different candidate keys for the `user` table. A *candidate key* is the smallest possible combination of attributes that can uniquely identify a row in a table. *Smallest* means that no subpart of a candidate key can uniquely identify a row. The combination of `username` and `first_name`, for example, can identify a row uniquely, but `username`, when used as a subpart of this combination, can also identity a row uniquely. Therefore, the combination of `username` and `first_name` is not a candidate key. On the other hand, `username` is a candidate key.

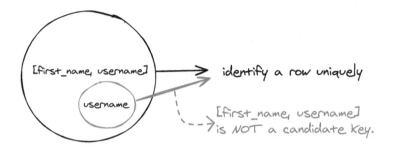

Can you take a systematic approach to identifying candidate keys? Yes. You start by examining each attribute to see whether it can identify a row uniquely. If you can't find such an attribute, start combining columns to see whether they can identify a row uniquely. In our case, the `user` table contains three candidate keys: `username`, `email`, and `phone_number`. To pick one primary key, you must compare their qualities:

	(username)	(email)	(phone_number)
unique	✓	✓	✓
Non-empty (null)	✓	✓	✗
Stable	✗	✓	✓
Simple	✓	✓	✓
Short	✓	✗	✓
Familiar	✓	✓	✓
Preventing redundancy	✓	✓	✓

The preceding list is not exhaustive but serves as a general guideline. The meanings of these requirements are clear. *Stable*, for example, means not likely to change, and *simple* means easy to understand and use. The *unique* and *nonempty* (non-nullability) requirements are satisfied almost by default in `username` and `email`. The `phone_number` values might be NULL because even if a customer doesn't have or doesn't want to give us a phone number, we still welcome that customer to register as a user.

The rest of the metrics can be quite subjective. Usernames, for example, can be easier to change than email addresses; on the other hand, email addresses tend to be longer, which affects access speed. In our case, we will settle on email as the primary key for the user table because of its stability. The Sci-Fi Collective allows users to update their usernames but not their email addresses, and updates to primary key values are strongly discouraged. You can indicate which attribute is the primary key by underlining it or adding a key symbol to its left:

Consider another example. Among the seven attributes and their possible combinations in the product table, you can identify at least two candidate keys:

- *Product codes*—In the real world, most products have product codes, which can help identify products uniquely. Because each product has a unique code, the code can also prevent redundancy.
- *Product names and manufacturers*—The combination of product names and manufacturers can also uniquely identify products and prevent redundancy in the product table.

The following figure compares these candidate keys:

	(code)	(name, manufacturer)
unique	✓	✓
Non-empty (null)	✓	✓
Stable	✓	✓
Simple	✓	✗
Short	✓	✗
Familiar	✗	✓
Preventing redundancy	✓	✓

The product code is a clear winner over the combination of product name and manufacturer. The product code is simpler and shorter.

Although the concept of the product code may be less familiar, it is not difficult to grasp. The product code is based on the Universal Product Code (UPC), unique 12-digit numbers assigned to each product sold in stores and online around the world. So you can settle for `product_code` and use it as the primary key for the `product` table:

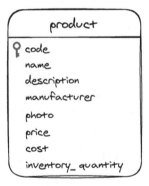

In both examples, we picked the primary key from a set of candidate keys. What if no candidate key is available or is a good fit? We will answer this question by picking a primary key for the `review` table, which has two columns: `review_text` and `review_time`. Neither of the two columns can uniquely identify a row in the `review` table. Although the combination of `review_text` and `review_time` can identify rows uniquely in most cases, it is still possible for two reviews with the same text to be recorded at the same time. That said, no candidate key is available for the `review` table:

	(review_txt)	(review_time)	(review_txt, review_time)
unique	✗	✗	✗
Non-empty (null)	✓	✓	✓
Stable	✗	✓	✗
Simple	✗	✗	✗
Short	✗	✗	✗
Familiar	✓	✓	✓
Preventing redundancy	✗	✗	✗

When you are in a situation like this one, always think about the alternative: creating a new column and using it as the primary key. You can opt to create a numeric column and use it as the primary key for the `review` table. Numeric primary keys are smaller and can fit completely in computer memory, making them much faster to search. They also scale better and are more standardized than a combination of two attributes. We will create an autoincrementing numeric attribute, `review_id`, and use it as the primary key for the `review` table. This type of key is known as a *surrogate key*.

Undoubtedly, a surrogate key can identify rows in a table uniquely. But can such a key prevent redundancy? Well, not by itself. It is still possible for two identical rows of data to be inserted into the `review` table, as shown in the following figure:

review_id	review_text	review_time
...	...	...
7	"Great product"	"9/14/2024, 9:15:15 AM"
8	"Great product"	"9/14/2024, 9:15:15 AM"

Would redundancy be a problem? For tables such as `user` and `product`, it is important to eliminate redundancy. Think about maintaining two rows of data that represent the same user. Which row should be used when the user updates their username? By contrast, reviews are always displayed as lists of texts on the same screen. As long as a row of review data can be identified uniquely, it can be updated or deleted properly. Therefore, redundancy won't be much of a problem for the `review` table.

Following the same logic, you see that the `payment_method` and `purchase` tables are in a similar situation: identifying each row uniquely is more important than eliminating redundancy. For the `purchase` table, redundancy is tolerable. The `purchase` table represents the transaction records of users. A transaction record is immutable. For the `payment_method` table, redundancy is not only tolerable but also acceptable. The Sci-Fi Collective allows two different users to add the same payment method to their individual accounts. (Think about when a couple uses each other's credit cards.)

In such a scenario, autoincrementing surrogate keys are a great choice for the primary keys. We will name the surrogate keys `payment_id` in the `payment_method` table and `purchase_id` in the `purchase` table. The following figure shows the primary keys of all entities:

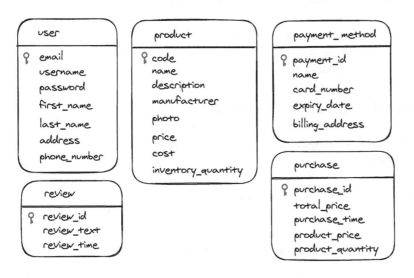

Superkeys, candidate keys, and primary keys

Another type of key that we haven't mentioned yet is the superkey. A *superkey* is a set of one or more columns of a table that can uniquely identify a row in the table. But—shame on the superkey—it may contain columns that aren't required to uniquely identify a row.

Now you know what superkeys are, you can see candidate keys from a different angle: a candidate key is a minimal superkey, which means that it has no unnecessary columns.

Finally, of all the candidate keys in a table, one is chosen as the primary key. The following figure shows the relationships among the three types of keys:

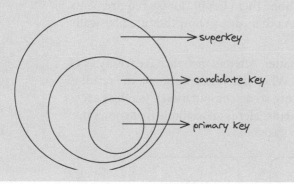

Data types

You successfully identified or generated the primary keys of all entities in the preceding section. In this section, you will work to define data types for all attributes—a necessary step toward completing your design of entities and attributes. To implement the database based on your design, you need the data types of attributes.

Data types are not an entirely new topic. In chapters 1 and 2, you saw how data types are used in SQL queries. In chapter 3, you were encouraged to get sample data that helps you figure out the data types of the characteristics of subjects in the requirements-gathering phase. In this section, you will take advantage of the sample data you accumulated and use it to define data types of all attributes accurately. Meanwhile, you will pick up some new conceptual knowledge of data types.

String data types: Power of personality

String data types are among the most-used data types in databases. Before you use string data types, you will learn a little bit about their variations.

CHAR, VARCHAR, and TEXT

The most common types of string data are CHAR, VARCHAR, and TEXT. The major difference among them lies in storage requirements. (Some require more bytes than others due to how they are physically implemented, for example.)

You may wonder why bytes matter. After all, people have terabytes of available space on their disks. When databases are small, the result is negligible, but as databases grow, so do computational (such as access speed) and memory requirements. Here's an example that shows the effect of data length on search speed:

<table>
<tr><td>

1
2
3
4
5
6
7
8

</td><td>

1,231,321,546
3,321,547,542
3,432,786,876
5,456,789,342
1,546,898,321
7,546,768,853
2,345,657,789
9,324,546,768

</td></tr>
</table>

Please try finding the number 8 in the left figure; then try finding 1,546,898,321 in the right figure. If it took you even a millisecond longer to find the longer number, congratulations: you are no different from a computer. Your choice of data types may cause data to bloat, which in turn slows data lookups (such as SELECT) and other operations.

Now that you know that bytes matter, we can present some simple guidelines for choosing a string data type:

- When an attribute has data of uniform length, use CHAR.
- When an attribute has data of a relatively short but varied length, use VARCHAR. *Relatively short* here also implies that an upper limit can be easily estimated (such as 500 characters).
- When an attribute is expected to have a large amount of text data that regularly exceeds a few thousand characters (1,000 plus), use TEXT, especially if the upper limit is hard to estimate.

Some examples can help demonstrate these guidelines. If you need an attribute to store state/province data as part of the address information of your customers in the United States and Canada, you can use a two-character designation (such as WA for Washington state). CHAR is the perfect data type for this attribute. As another example, if you need an attribute to store users' names, you can expect data length to vary. Also, you can estimate the upper limit of the names; most names don't need to go beyond 30 characters. Therefore, VARCHAR is the perfect data type for this attribute. The following figure summarizes these two examples:

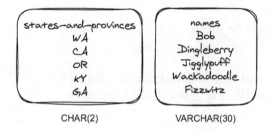

In the preceding figure, you may notice that CHAR and VARCHAR are followed by parentheses with numbers in them. This syntax deserves some explanation. When you use CHAR or VARCHAR to define data types, you need to declare the length. CHAR(2) indicates that each data record of this attribute will occupy exactly 2 bytes. VARCHAR(30) indicates that each data record of its attribute can occupy up to 30 characters. In some RDBMSs, such as MySQL, a record can be rejected or truncated when its character length exceeds the declared length.

As for the data type TEXT, it is typically used to hold a large amount of text data, such as a product description, a product manual, or book text.

Strings and database performance

In some databases, TEXT may not be stored inline along with the rest of the columns; instead, the data may exist in secondary file storage, requiring further lookups and a performance delay. Use this data type sparingly and only when necessary (for description fields, for example).

Also, text attributes are indexable through full-text indexes (specialized indexes for larger text that work like a search engine), which are not supported by all database systems. Before version 5.6, for example, MySQL had no support for this feature in its InnoDB engine. In such cases, all searches on text attributes have to be linear and therefore will be slow. If the string data in an attribute is short, and if you expect this attribute to be searched frequently, VARCHAR is the better choice of data type.

Identify string attributes in our database

Now that you have learned the basics of string data types, you are ready to identify the attributes in our database for which string data types are a good fit. To complete this task, you will do the following for each entity:

1. Check the requirements and the sample data that you got from the requirements-gathering phase.
2. Identify the attributes that should be strings.
3. Choose a string data type (CHAR, VARCHAR, or TEXT).

First, you check the requirements and sample data. Our user entity, for example, has seven attributes. The following figure shows the sample data for this entity:

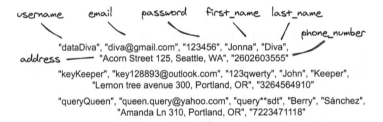

Next, you identify attributes that should be strings. From the sample data, you can tell that all the attributes are strings. In other words, all seven attributes are string data types.

Finally, you choose a string data type for the identified attributes. From the sample data, you can tell that all attributes have variable lengths, and it is not difficult to estimate the maximum length for these variables. Therefore, VARCHAR is the most appropriate data type. A phone number, for example, cannot contain more than 15 digits (excluding formatting) no matter where you are, thanks to the international phone numbering plan. Therefore, the data type of phone_number would be VARCHAR(15).

You may wonder whether storing the passwords as plain text using VARCHAR would introduce a security problem. Of course it will! We will address security-related challenges in chapter 7. For now, VARCHAR is good enough.

When you identify all the data types of the attribute, you can put the data type to the right of the attribute to complete your design of the `user` entity:

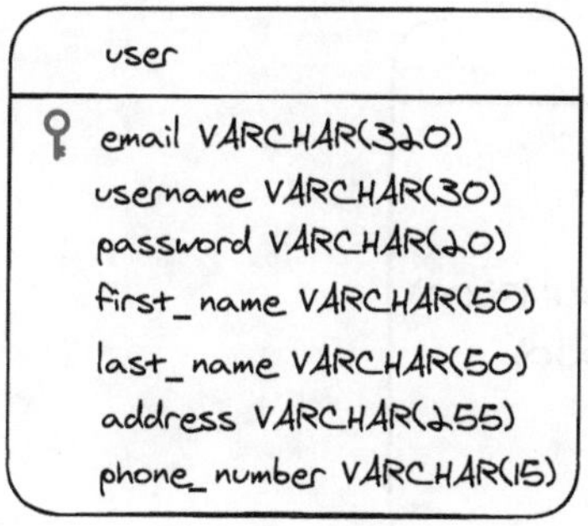

In case you have difficulty estimating a reasonable character limit for a VARCHAR attribute, always ask the domain experts or developers follow-up questions. When you don't have access to them, at least consult ChatGPT. A question like the following can help you learn a lot:

What's the maximum length of common names?``

Now let's turn our focus to the `product` entity. The following figure shows the sample data for the `product` entity:

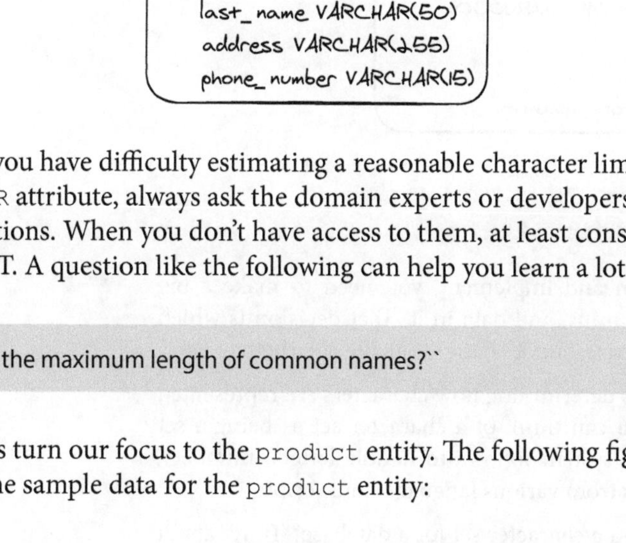

From the sample data, you can tell that all four attributes are strings. VARCHAR is good enough for the `name` and `manufacturer` attributes. But you can expect product descriptions and photo URLs to be long strings—especially product descriptions. To be safe, you can assign TEXT to the description attribute. Considering that the photo URLs won't be unreasonably long, you can stick to VARCHAR but declare a length that can accommodate URLs up to 1,000 characters. The updated product entity looks like this:

Lost in translation: Character sets

In every database you design and implement, you need to make a big decision about the tables, columns, and data in it. That decision is which character set to use for a database, and it's better to make it early than late.

A *character set* is a set of rules determining how characters are represented and stored in a database. You can think of a character set as being a set of guidelines that a database system follows to handle letters, numbers, symbols, and other characters from various languages and scripts.

Why do you need to decide on a character set for a database? Think about human languages around the world; different languages use different letters and characters. English uses the letters A, B, C, and so on, whereas Chinese uses characters that look very different. Different character sets support different languages. There are character sets for Latin-based languages (such as Latin1), as well as character sets for internationalization and multilingual content (such as UTF-8). When you design a database, it's important to choose a character set that aligns with the languages and symbols you'll be working with to ensure data accuracy and compatibility.

You typically decide on the character set when you create a database is created, which is why it's best to make the decision early. Some RDBMS may not allow you to change the character set, and even if you can, changing character sets can be complex and may result in data loss or corruption.

What about the other entities? Feel free to pause reading and try to identify and define their string attributes. If you are pressed for time, here are the declared string attributes for all entities:

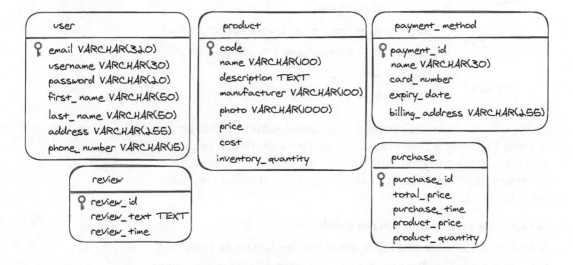

Integers: Number your way to success

Before you can use integer data types fluently, you need to learn a little bit about them.

TINYINT, SMALLINT, MEDIUMINT, INT, and BIGINT

The most common types of integer data are TINYINT, SMALLINT, INT, and BIGINT. These data types allocate a fixed number of bytes based on a power of 2 and are 1, 2, 4, and 8 bytes, respectively. Also, these data types have different minimum and maximum values, which vary depending on whether they are set up as signed or unsigned.

In some database systems, an unsigned number doesn't have a + or – sign associated with it. In other words, an unsigned number cannot be negative. By contrast, a signed number can be negative. The ranges of the four integer types, signed and unsigned, are shown in the following figure.

$$
\text{TINYINT} \begin{cases} \text{signed} & : -128 \text{ to } 127 \\ \text{unsigned} & : 0 \text{ to } 255 \end{cases}
$$

$$
\text{SMALLINT} \begin{cases} \text{signed} & : -32{,}768 \text{ to } 32{,}767 \\ \text{unsigned} & : 0 \text{ to } 65{,}535 \end{cases}
$$

$$
\text{INT} \begin{cases} \text{signed} & : -2{,}147{,}483{,}648 \text{ to } 2{,}147{,}483{,}647 \ (\sim 2 \text{ billion}) \\ \text{unsigned} & : 0 \text{ to } 4{,}294{,}967{,}295 \ (\sim 4 \text{ billion}) \end{cases}
$$

$$
\text{BIGINT} \begin{cases} \text{signed} & : -2^{63} \text{ to } 2^{63} - 1 \\ \text{unsigned} & : 0 \text{ to } 2^{64} \end{cases}
$$

As you can see, TINYINT can hold a maximum value of 255 as unsigned but only 127 as signed. INT can accommodate a maximum value as 4,294,967,295 as unsigned, which is big. But if you have a numeric attribute with a data value that can be bigger than 4 billion, you need the help of BIGINT.

Identify integer attributes in our database

Now that you have learned the basics of integer data types, you are ready to identify the attributes for which integer data types are a good fit in our database.

To complete this task, you will follow the same procedure you used to identify string attributes. Start by examining the requirements and sample data that you got from the requirements-gathering phase; then identify the integer attributes and choose an appropriate integer data type for each attribute.

First, focus your attention on the ID attributes. Numeric IDs are stable, unique, simple, and efficient. Following this logic, you can declare the payment_id attribute as an integer attribute, for example. You need to decide among the different types of integer data types, of course. It is self-evident that TINYINT is too small and thus not a good fit. If you aim to build a super online store that sells products across the galaxy, SMALLINT is also too small and not a good fit. BIGINT would work well and is big enough. But you can comfortably settle on INT because INT is big enough for now and yields comparatively better database performance. (The fewer bytes are used, the faster the SELECT query will be, for example.) Although whether an integer attribute is signed or unsigned is rarely reflected in an entity-relationship (E-R) diagram, you still need to make that choice. All primary keys have no reason to have negative values, so they are unsigned.

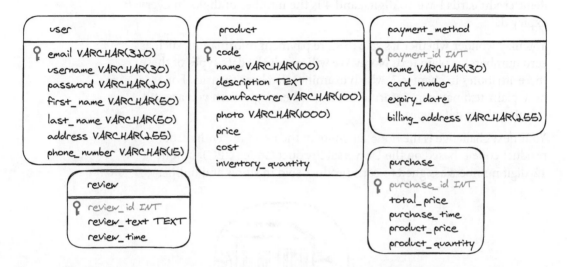

Most integer attributes in our database are easy to identify, but there are two tricky cases: the `payment_method` entity and the `code` attribute in the `product` entity. Here is the `payment_method` entity in the requirements-gathering phase:

```
name      card_number   expiry_date
   \           \             \
"master card", 5260405254103227, 0227, ...
"boa visa", 3169596072241198,1225, ...
"amex", 1677288846463190, 1129, ...
```

The values of both `card_number` and `expiry_date` seem to be integers in the sample data, but we recommend that you define them as strings instead of integers. This case is one in which you have to sacrifice storage efficiency for clarity, practicality, and correctness. Because no mathematical operations are performed on information such as debit/credit card numbers and expiry dates, you don't need to make the values integers. What's more, making them integers will cause unnecessary problems because a card number or expiry date may have leading zeros. In numerical data types, the leading zeros are eliminated, so such information would not be stored correctly. As a result, you should define the data type of card numbers as CHAR(16) and expiry_date as CHAR(4), where 16 is the number of digits: all debit/credit cards have 16 digits, and 4 is the number of digits in every expiry date.

You may wonder whether it's safe to store payment information, such as card numbers, as plain text. Nope. We will revisit the data types of these three attributes in chapter 7, which examines database security. For now, plain-text payment information is good enough when you are still learning about data types.

Your next challenge is the code attribute in the product entity. The product code is based on the Universal Product Code (UPC), unique 12-digit numbers assigned to each product sold in stores and online.

For the same reasons (leading zeros), it is more appropriate to define the data type of code as a string than as an integer. Because all UPC values have the same length, 12 digits, we can define the code attribute as CHAR(12).

You can identify other integer attributes and define their data types the same way. You should think about the maximum practical value of giving an integer attribute a specific integer type. This approach will help keep your database small and efficient in the long run. Here's what the remaining integer attributes look like for all entities:

```
┌─────────────────────────────────┐   ┌─────────────────────────────────────┐   ┌──────────────────────────────────────┐
│ user                            │   │ product                             │   │ payment_method                       │
├─────────────────────────────────┤   ├─────────────────────────────────────┤   ├──────────────────────────────────────┤
│ ⚲ email varchar(320)            │   │ ⚲ code CHAR(12)                     │   │ ⚲ payment_id INT                     │
│   username VARCHAR(30)          │   │   name VARCHAR(100)                 │   │   name VARCHAR(30)                   │
│   password VARCHAR(20)          │   │   description TEXT                  │   │   card_number CHAR(16)               │
│   first_name VARCHAR(50)        │   │   manufacturer VARCHAR(100)         │   │   expiry_date CHAR(4)                │
│   last_name VARCHAR(50)         │   │   photo VARCHAR(1000)               │   │   billing_address VARCHAR(255)       │
│   address VARCHAR(255)          │   │   price                             │   └──────────────────────────────────────┘
│   phone_number VARCHAR(15)      │   │   cost                              │
└─────────────────────────────────┘   │   inventory_quantity INT            │   ┌──────────────────────────────────────┐
                                       └─────────────────────────────────────┘   │ purchase                             │
   ┌─────────────────────────────┐                                               ├──────────────────────────────────────┤
   │ review                      │                                               │ ⚲ purchase_id INT                    │
   ├─────────────────────────────┤                                               │   total_price                        │
   │ ⚲ review_id INT             │                                               │   purchase_time                      │
   │   review_text TEXT          │                                               │   product_price                      │
   │   review_time               │                                               │   product_quantity INT               │
   └─────────────────────────────┘                                               └──────────────────────────────────────┘
```

Float like a butterfly, decimal like a data queen

In the preceding section, you may have noticed that we did not assign
an integer data type to the `price` attribute of the `product` entity. You
may wonder what data types are more appropriate for this attribute and
others like it. The answer is decimals. Before you can use decimal data
types fluently, you need to learn a little bit about them.

Floating-point vs. fixed-point data types

You have two choices for declaring a decimal attribute: *floating-
point* types and *fixed-point* types. Common floating-point data types
include `FLOAT` and `DOUBLE`. `FLOAT` is typically 32-bit, and `DOUBLE`
is typically 64-bit. In other words, `DOUBLE` can accommodate bigger
numbers. `FLOAT` and `DOUBLE` are used widely when accuracy is not
strictly required, as in sensor reading, statistical analysis, and physical
simulation. When accuracy is required to the extent that you should
care about every decimal value, you should avoid the `FLOAT` and
`DOUBLE` data types due to the need for finite precision and the potential
for rounding errors.

Suppose that you have a database that keeps track of money exchanges
through different currencies for its users. (Handling other people's
money is fun.)

If you want to convert 1,000,001 USD to EUR with an exchange rate of 0.83, rounding errors in a 32-bit floating-point operation may result in 830000.8125. This result is about 1.75 euro cents less than it should be. This difference may not seem like much, but users of such a system will lose money for no reason, especially frequent users and those who transfer huge amounts of money.

$$\$1,000,001 \xrightarrow{\ \$1 \times 0.83€\ } \begin{array}{l} \text{Actual: } 830000.83 \\ \text{32-bit Float: } 830000.8125 \\ \text{Error: } -0.0175 \end{array}$$

Now that you have a rough idea of what we mean by *accuracy*, let's define the word formally before moving further. *Accuracy* means specific requirements for precision and scale. *Precision* refers to the total number of significant digits, and *scale* refers to the number of digits stored to the right of the decimal point. Consider the number 12.3456: its precision is 6, and its scale is 4.

Scale Here: 4

$$12 . \overbrace{}^{} 3456$$

$$\underbrace{12 . 3456}_{}$$

Precision   Here: 6

When accuracy is required, you should think about fixed-point data types such as DECIMAL and NUMERIC. There are no real differences between DECIMAL and NUMERIC in many RDBMSs, such as MySQL and PostgreSQL. In such cases, you can use either data type. If you are not sure whether the RDBMS you use falls into this category, refer to its documentation or check with ChatGPT.

Identify decimal attributes in our database

Now that you know the basics of decimal data types, you are ready to identify the decimal attributes in our database. To complete this task, you will follow the same procedure that you used to identify string and integer attributes. To identify the decimal attributes in the product table, for example, take a look at the sample product data:

name   description   manufacturer   price   cost

"Atomic Nose Hair Trimmer", "Trim your nose ...", "Mad Inventors Inc.", 19.99, 9.99, ...

"Selfie Toaster", "Get your face on ...", "Goofy Gadgets Corp", 24.99, 15.02, ...

"Cat-Poop Coffee", "The only coffee made", "Absurd Accessories", 29.99, 21.85, ...

Do you see the values for the price and cost attributes? They represent money. In other words, they require accuracy, so you should think about using DECIMAL. For money, it makes sense for the scale to be 2 because that's the smallest unit of money (cents). In larger monetary operations, a higher scale may be necessary to accommodate for roundoff operations. All our products sell for less than $1,000, so precision can comfortably stay as 7:

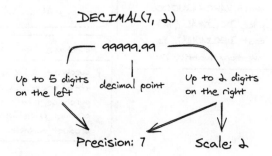

Therefore, you define the data type of both the price and cost attributes as DECIMAL(7, 2), where 7 specifies the precision and 2 specifies the scale. You can update your design of the product entity accordingly:

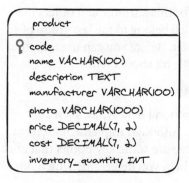

You can apply the same steps to identify decimal attributes in other tables—essentially any other attributes that are money-related, such as the product_price and the total_price attributes in purchase. If you worry that a single transaction may lead to a large bill, you can increase precision for the total_price attribute, such as DECIMAL(13, 2). The following figure shows the updated design of all the entities.

user
- 🔑 email VARCHAR(320)
- username VARCHAR(30)
- password VARCHAR(20)
- first_name VARCHAR(50)
- last_name VARCHAR(50)
- address VARCHAR(255)
- phone_number VARCHAR(15)

product
- 🔑 code CHAR(12)
- name VARCHAR(100)
- description TEXT
- manufacturer VARCHAR(100)
- photo VARCHAR(1000)
- price DECIMAL(7, 2)
- cost DECIMAL(7, 2)
- inventory_quantity INT

payment_method
- 🔑 payment_id INT
- name VARCHAR(30)
- card_number CHAR(16)
- expiry_date CHAR(4)
- billing_address VARCHAR(255)

purchase
- 🔑 purchase_id INT
- total_price DECIMAL(13, 2)
- purchase_time
- product_price DECIMAL(7, 2)
- product_quantity INT

review
- 🔑 review_id INT
- review_text TEXT
- review_time

Temporal data types: Time flies when you're querying

In the preceding section, you may have noticed that we did not assign any data types to the `review_time` attribute of the `review` entity. You may wonder what data types are appropriate for this attribute and others like it. The answer is temporal data types, which belong to the last group of data types you learned about in this chapter. Before you can use temporal data types fluently, you need to learn a little bit about them.

DATE, TIME, DATETIME, and TIMESTAMP

Most database systems support some temporal data types, such as `DATE`, `TIME`, `DATETIM`, and `TIMESTAMP`. Although implementations of such data types vary across RDBMSs, here are some key points that are consistent across most systems and can help you determine which one to use:

- Use `DATE` when a date needs to be stored without any time information, such as birthday data. The date `'1980-05-15'` represents May 15, 1980, for example.
- Use `TIME` when only time needs to be stored. If you want to track the time at which events occur during the day, you can use the `TIME` data type. The time `'14:30:00'` represents 2:30 p.m., for example.

- Use DATETIME when both date and time information need to be stored to represent historical time, future events, or other instances in which the time zone is an inherent part of the time and should not be adjusted.
- Use TIMESTAMP to record the exact moment of an event that needs to be consistent across time zones, such as log timestamps, record creation, and modification times. Typically, the RDBMS handles the conversion of time zones in TIMESTAMP data automatically.

If you are designing a database for an application whose users are strictly local, such as an ordering system for a restaurant, you don't need to worry about time-zone problems. But if you are building an application that might be used around the globe, you may wonder whether the time-zone data will be stored as part of the temporal data attributes. Regardless of the specifics of the RDBMS, you should consider storing date and time values in *Coordinated Universal Time* (UTC) because it ensures consistency and prevents problems with Daylight Saving Time changes, different time zones, and traveling users.

UTC is like a big clock that everyone agrees to follow. It's the same time for everyone, no matter where they are. If you live in Seattle, and your friends in Beijing want to let you know their local time without explicitly giving you the exact time, they can say "Our local time is UTC plus 8 hours." You can not only calculate their local time but also compare their time with yours because you know how your local time compares with UTC. That said, any web or mobile applications can calculate local time given a UTC time.

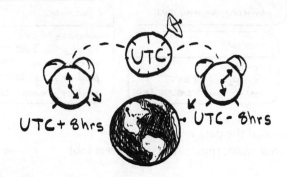

Identify attributes representing date and time in our database

Now you are ready to identify the attributes that represent date and time in our database. To complete this task, follow the same steps you used to declare data types in earlier sections. You start by referring to sample data you collected in the requirements-gathering phase. In this case, however, you may find the task trivial because the attributes related to date and time have self-revealing names (that is, *time* is part of the name).

Two attributes are related to date and time: the `review_time` attribute in `review` and the `purchase_time` attribute in `purchase`. During the requirements-gathering phase, you learned that both attributes require date and time information because they represent exact moments of some events that need to be consistent across time zones. Thus, you can declare the data type of both attributes as `TIMESTAMP`.

Also, you learned that you need to track the last time a user accessed the online store by adding another `TIMESTAMP` attribute to the `user` entity and naming it `last_login_time`. With all these updates, here is another version of the updated entities:

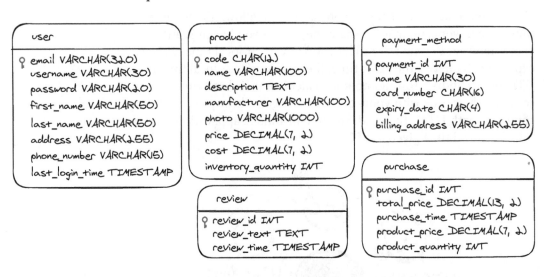

So far, you have successfully identified the data types of all the attributes. Take another look at your masterpiece. You did a great job!

Inconsistencies of data types across RDBMSs

Like it or not, there are inconsistencies of data types across RDBMSs. The data types that you have learned are common across RDBMSs, but you need to learn about exceptions and particularities in individual systems. The entities and attributes you developed in this chapter are perfect for MySQL, MariaDB, and PostgreSQL, but you will need to make small or big adjustments for other RDBMSs for the following reasons:

- In SQLite, it is common to use `TEXT` in place of `TIMESTAMP`.

- Oracle uses `NUMBER` in place of `INT` and `DECIMAL` and `VARCHAR2` in place of `TEXT`.

- SQL Server uses `NVARCHAR(MAX)` in place of `TEXT` and `DATETIME2` or `DATETIMEOFFSET` in place of `TIMESTAMP`.

You can find such information in the GitHub repository that accompanies this book.

Recap

- Designing an entity requires identifying all its attributes, the primary key, and the data types of all attributes.

- A primary key should be able to identify each row in a table uniquely. Depending on your case, you may need a primary key to prevent redundancies. If no candidate key is available or a good fit, you can always create a numeric attribute and use it as the primary key.

- Common data types in databases include string, integer, decimal, and temporal. To decide which data type to use, think about what job a data type is good for as well as the demands of your particular case.

- Given an attribute, to identify its data type, you need to examine the sample data and the information collected during the requirements-gathering phase, identify the proper data-type group (such as string), and choose the best fit within that group (such as TEXT) based on the maximum allowed values or spaces derived from your requirements analysis.
- Using proper data types ensures that a database stores data efficiently and meets the demands of data querying.

In this chapter

- You establish relationships between entities.

- You identify the cardinality of each relationship.

- You decide whether to represent some entities as weak entities.

What you need to know

You can find the database design covered in this chapter implemented in tools commonly used by practitioners, such as dbdiagram.io and MySQL Workbench, in the GitHub repository (https://github.com/Neo-Hao/grokking-relational-database-design). You can navigate to the `chapter_05` folder and follow the instructions in `README.md` to load the database design into corresponding tools.

The data types that show up in this chapter apply to most relational database management systems (RDBMSs), such as MySQL, MariaDB, and PostgreSQL. If you use another RDBMS, such as SQL Server or SQLite, you may need to make small modifications to the design by replacing certain data types with equivalents specific to the target RDBMS. You can find such information in `README.md` in the `chapter_05` folder.

Overview

In this chapter, you will develop your entity-relationship (E-R) diagram for The Sci-Fi Collective's online store by establishing relationships among entities you identified in chapter 4. By doing so, you will learn important database design concepts, such as cardinality and dependency.

Entity-relationship diagrams

E-R diagrams are graphical representations of entities and their relationships in a database. E-R diagrams are not only visual tools but also documents that describe database structures and rules. Over the years, these diagrams have become a universal design language among database designers.

An E-R diagram is typically composed of boxes representing the entities and lines representing the relationships among the entities. The diagram depicts the data structure (also known as the *data schema*) but not the data. In an E-R diagram, a table with millions of records is still represented as a single entity. The E-R diagram that you will develop by the end of this chapter looks like this:

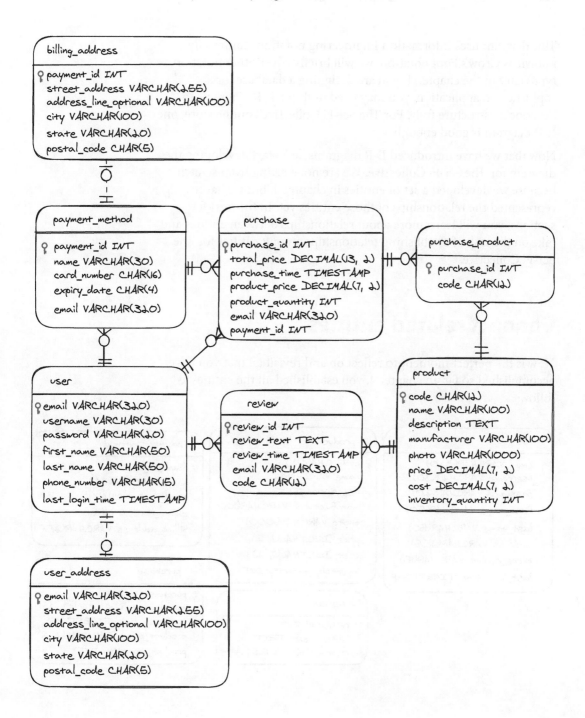

This diagram uses Information Engineering notation, commonly known as Crow's Foot notation; we will briefly cover other notation types later in the chapter. If you are designing a database for a sophisticated application, you may need multiple E-R diagrams to describe its structure fully. For The Sci-Fi Collective's online store, one E-R diagram is good enough.

Now that we have introduced E-R diagrams, let's start developing the diagram for The Sci-Fi Collective. We are not starting from scratch because we developed a set of entities in chapter 4, but we haven't represented the relationships of those entities yet. In the next few sections, you will learn more about relationships between entities and take on the task of establishing relationships among entities for The Sci-Fi Collective.

Connect related entities

Now is the perfect moment to reflect on and revisit all that you have accomplished so far. In chapter 4, you established all the entities as follows:

user
🔑 email VARCHAR(320)
username VARCHAR(30)
password VARCHAR(20)
first_name VARCHAR(50)
last_name VARCHAR(50)
address VARCHAR(255)
phone_number VARCHAR(15)
last_login_time TIMESTAMP

product
🔑 code CHAR(12)
name VARCHAR(100)
description TEXT
manufacturer VARCHAR(100)
photo VARCHAR(1000)
price DECIMAL(7, 2)
cost DECIMAL(7, 2)
inventory_quantity INT

payment_method
🔑 payment_id INT
name VARCHAR(30)
card_number CHAR(16)
expiry_date CHAR(4)
billing_address VARCHAR(255)

review
🔑 review_id INT
review_text TEXT
review_time TIMESTAMP

purchase
🔑 purchase_id INT
total_price DECIMAL(13, 2)
purchase_time TIMESTAMP
product_price DECIMAL(7, 2)
product_quantity INT

In chapter 3, you went over the requirements-gathering phase and collected useful information that pertains to the relationships among the preceding entities. You copied this information:

- A *user* can *make* multiple *purchases*; an order can be made by only one user.

- A *user* can *review* multiple *products* as long as the user bought those products; a product can be reviewed by multiple users.

- A *user* can *maintain* multiple *payment methods*; a payment method can be associated with only one user.

- A *purchase* can *have* more than one *product*; a product can show up in multiple orders.

In an E-R diagram, you use a line to connect every pair of two entities that are related. To establish relationships between two entities, you will identify every relationship and connect every pair of related entities using lines.

Your first step in connecting entities is synthesizing the information you gathered and the design of entities. Your goal is to generate a list of simple sentences composed only of subjects, verbs, and objects. The sentences will help you understand the relationships between every pair of entities. As you designed entities, you may have introduced changes that conflicted with the gathered information. You designed a `review`

entity, for example, but it didn't appear as a noun in the information you gathered. To reconcile such conflicts, think about whether it makes sense to keep the `review` entity. If so, adapt the synthesized information accordingly:

- A user makes purchases.
- A user writes reviews.
- A product has reviews.
- A user maintains payment methods.
- A purchase contains products.

Next, map this summary to a diagram. The nouns in every sentence represent entities. If two nouns connected by some verbs show up in one sentence, the two entities are+ likely to be related. You may go through a few iterations of trial and error when mapping the summary to a diagram because of possible inaccuracy and misinterpretation. When you draw an entity in your draft E-R diagram, you can skip the attributes for now because they don't matter yet and listing all of them is tedious. Based on the preceding summary, you will develop the following draft diagram:

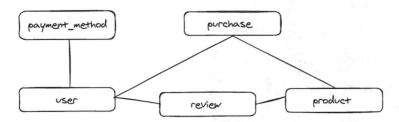

When you generate a draft diagram, you should test every relationship against the information you gathered and the sample data you collected. Also, take the draft diagram to the stakeholders and explain your design rationale to them because it is likely that you made some mistakes or neglected something critical in your first few iterations. The software developers of The Sci-Fi Collective, for example, will point out that an online purchase can't be performed without a payment method. Based on the new information, you need to answer the following question before revising the draft diagram:

Should `payment_method` be related to `purchase`?

Without the payment method information, an online order can't be finished, and the online store can't bill its users. In other words, each purchase record needs to be mapped to a corresponding payment method. Therefore, a relationship between `payment_method` and `purchase` makes sense. With this question answered, add one more relationship:

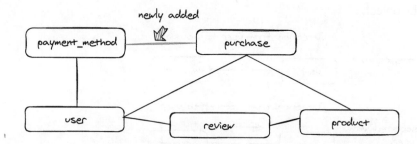

In the next two sections, you will learn more about the characteristics of a relationship between two entities, which will empower you to develop the draft diagram further.

Cardinality

Cardinality is an important characteristic of a relationship between two entities, describing the number of instances of one entity that can be associated with a single instance of another entity via the relationship. Based on that definition, cardinality is classified into several types, each of which is represented differently in an E-R diagram.

To complete your E-R diagram, you need to analyze the information you collected from the requirements-gathering phase, identify the cardinality of each relationship, and update the draft diagram accordingly.

Direction and representation

If you consider directions, a relationship between two entities can be broken into two directional relationships. In a banking system, for example, `user` and `account` are two entities, and their relationship(s) can be summarized using two sentences:

- *Sentence 1*—A user has zero, one, or more accounts.
- *Sentence 2*—An account is associated with one and only one user.

Sentences 1 and 2 represent two different directional relationships between `user` and `account`. In both sentences, the direction flows from the subject to the object:

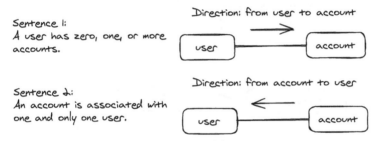

Given a directional relationship from A to B, cardinality describes the number of instances of B with which a single instance of A can be associated. Cardinality is represented by two graphic symbols on the relationship line between A and B. The symbols are used in pairs to represent the cardinalities. The symbol on the inner side represents the minimum instance number of B that a single instance of A needs to be associated with—the *min cardinality*. The symbol on the outer side represents the maximum instance number of B that a single instance of A needs to be associated with—the *max cardinality*.

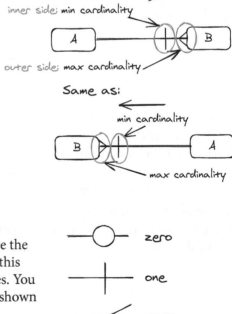

As you see in the preceding figure, to represent the cardinality of the relationship from A to B, you place the two symbols closer to B on the relationship line. In this example, the individual symbols represent quantities. You need to know the symbols for zero, one, and many, shown in the figure to the right.

Cardinality notation: Complicated relationships with math symbols

There are several ways to notate the cardinality of a relationship. The two most popular are Chen notation and Crow's Foot notation. Chen notation has historic significance. Crow's Foot notation is simpler and more popular among professionals. In this book, we will stick to Crow's Foot notation.

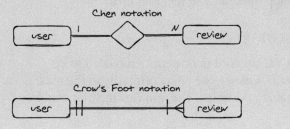

How do you represent the relationship cardinalities of the example you saw at the beginning of this section—the relationship between the `user` and `account` entities in a banking system?

- *Sentence 1*—A user has zero, one, or more accounts.
- *Sentence 2*—An account is associated with one and only one user.

The two sentences represent two directional relationships; they also contain the information you need to establish their cardinalities. Because a user is associated with zero, one, or more accounts, the min cardinality is zero, and the max cardinality is many for the relationship from `user` to `account`. Similarly, an account is associated with one and only one user, which means that both the max and min cardinalities for the relationship from `account` to `user` are one.

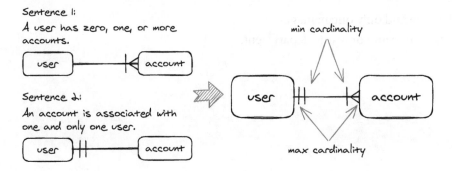

As you see in the preceding figure, you can merge the two directional relationships and use a single line to represent both. The cardinality symbols closer to `account` represent the cardinality of the relationship from `user` to `account`, whereas the symbols closer to `user` represent the cardinality of the relationship from `account` to `user`.

Now you know what cardinality is and how to represent it in E-R diagrams, you will learn about three common cardinality types and apply what you learn to develop the draft E-R diagram further.

One-to-one: A perfect match

In a one-to-one relationship, each record in one entity is related to up to one record in the other entity. *One-to-one* refers primarily to the max cardinality of both directional relationships. The min cardinalities could be either zero or one.

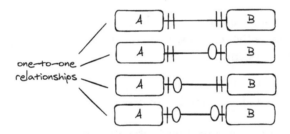

Given a one-to-one relationship, if both of the two min cardinalities are ones, one of the min cardinalities is typically converted to zero for easy implementation.

Consider an example. In the database of a large corporation, both departments and managers are represented, and their relationship is as follows:

- A department has one and only one manager.
- A manager works for one and only one department.

You can represent such a relationship in an E-R diagram as follows:

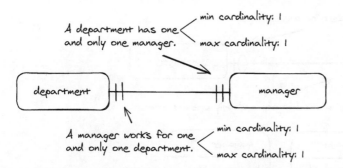

This representation is theoretically solid but impossible to implement. To link the two entities, you need help from foreign keys. If the two entities in the preceding figure have attributes, you need to place foreign keys in both tables because each department is associated with a manager and each manager is associated with a department:

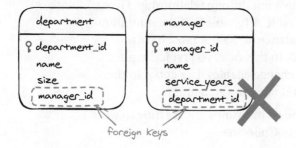

Such an implementation is problematic for data entry or insertion. When the two tables are created, they don't contain data, so you need to start populating the tables by entering department or manager information. If you enter a department record first, its manager data won't be available yet. The foreign key constraints you put in place cause SQL to complain and reject the data entry. If you switch the order and enter manager information first, you face the same problem. In such a situation, you can relax one of the two min cardinalities from one to zero to make implementation possible. You can modify the relationship between department and manager as follows:

- A department *has zero or one* manager.
- A manager works for one and only one department.

The representation and implementation are updated accordingly:

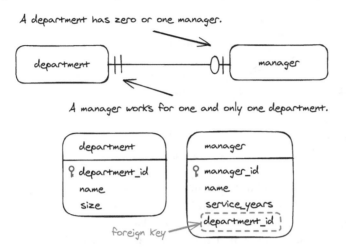

As you see in the preceding figure, the min cardinality can indicate where to place the foreign key in a one-to-one relationship. Given a directional relationship from table A to table B, if the minimum cardinality is zero, not every instance of table A must have a corresponding record in table B. In this case, you typically place the foreign key in table B. This change enables data entry. In this case, table A is `department`, and table B is `manager`.

Now you know what one-to-one relationships are, it's time to work on the E-R diagram of The Sci-Fi Collective.

Identify one-to-one relationships in your database

Based on the information you gathered in the requirements-gathering phase, you don't have a one-to-one relationship between the entities that you've identified. But some new information about users' addresses that you learned in the iterative process propels you to redesign your `user` entity. What is the problem? A user's address might look like this:

   20 Baldwin Rd, Shelter Island, New York, 11964

The data analysts of The Sci-Fi Collective need to filter users' data based on city, state/province, or zip code to conduct targeted marketing analysis from time to time. Storing users' address information in a VARCHAR attribute will make such a task difficult. To address this problem, factor the address information into a different entity with multiple attributes:

user

♀ email VARCHAR(320)
username VARCHAR(30)
password VARCHAR(20)
first_name VARCHAR(50)
last_name VARCHAR(50)
address VARCHAR(255)
phone_number VARCHAR(15)
last_login_time TIMESTAMP

user

♀ email VARCHAR(320)
username VARCHAR(30)
password VARCHAR(20)
first_name VARCHAR(50)
last_name VARCHAR(50)
phone_number VARCHAR(15)
last_login_time TIMESTAMP

user_address

♀ address_id INT
street_address VARCHAR(255)
address_line_optional VARCHAR(100)
city VARCHAR(100)
state VARCHAR(20)
postal_code CHAR(5)

As you can see, most of the attributes of this new entity (user_address) are of a string data type. You need to decide whether to assign CHAR or VARCHAR and their possible max lengths. To simplify the solution, assume that The Sci-Fi Collective operates only within the United States. This assumption will make it easier to determine the maximum lengths of all the string attributes. The state attribute, for example, can be assigned VARCHAR(20). North Carolina and South Carolina are among the longest state names (14 characters each). To be safe and accommodate any possible future changes, you can set the VARCHAR length 6 characters longer than 14. Or you can assign CHAR(5) to the postal_code attribute if you opt for the five-digit format.

Now that you have successfully converted the address attribute to a new entity, user_address, let's focus on the relationship between user and user_address. Here is the new information you gathered from the developer of The Sci-Fi Collective's online store:

- A user may not have an address when they first register an account, but a user must have one and only one address before making a purchase.
- An address is associated with only a single user.

Based on this information, you can easily determine the min and max cardinalities of the two directional relationships (from `user` to `user_address` and from `user_address` to `user`), and represent the merged relationship accordingly:

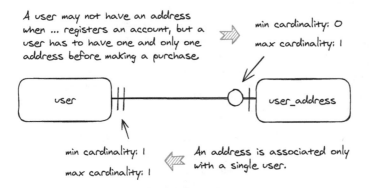

Is this relationship one-to-one? Yes. You may notice that the representation is similar to the example featuring departments and managers earlier in this chapter.

The representation of the relationship between `user` and `user_address` requires the help of a foreign key. As you learned in the preceding section, the min cardinality can indicate where the foreign key should be placed. In the directional relationship from `user` to `user_address`, the min cardinality is zero. Thus, you place the foreign key in the `user_address` entity:

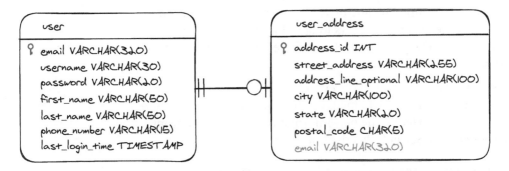

Now you know what a one-to-one relationship is and how to represent it, you should also know that one-to-one relationships are the rarest type because few one-to-one relationships exist in real life.

One-to-many: A love triangle

One-to-many relationships are the most common cardinality type. As in one-to-one relationships, *one-to-many* refers primarily to the max cardinalities. If two entities are related, one directional relationship has the max cardinality of one, and the other has the max cardinality of many.

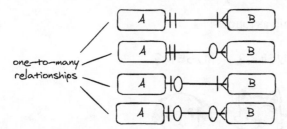

As you saw in the preceding section, if both min cardinalities are ones in one relationship, data entry will be problematic when the representation is implemented. In such a case, you typically relax the min cardinality of the many side from one to zero:

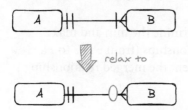

Let's deepen your understanding of a one-to-many relationship by looking at a real example, the relationship between the `user` and `review` entities in the draft diagram of The Sci-Fi Collective:

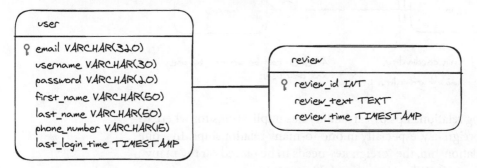

From the requirement-gathering phase and your follow-up inquiry on the relationship between the two entities, you managed to put together the following information:

- A user can write zero to many reviews.
- A review can be written by one and only user.

You can visualize this relationship as follows:

Based on this information, you can determine the min and max cardinalities of the two directional relationships (from `user` to `review` and from `review` to `user`), and represent the merged relationship accordingly:

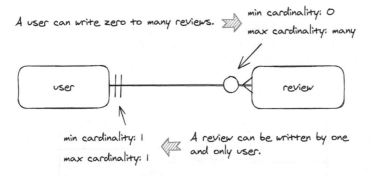

Categorizing relationships by cardinality has implications for where to place the foreign key, especially in one-to-many relationships. In a one-to-many relationship, the foreign key needs to be placed on the many side—the entity that the crow's foot (→) points to.

Why should the foreign key be placed on the many side of a one-to-many relationship? The many side may have multiple rows that correspond to one row on the one side via the foreign key. If you insist on putting the foreign key on the one side, the one side will need an extra row for each additional record from the corresponding many side, which is not possible.

In our case, the many side is the `review` entity. The foreign key in the `review` entity should be the primary key of the `user` entity. You can update the `review` entity accordingly:

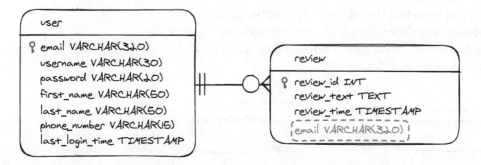

Identify one-to-many relationships in our database

Now you know what one-to-many relationships are, and you have updated the relationship between `user` and `review` entities in the draft diagram. You can apply your new knowledge by identifying other one-to-many relationships and updating them in the draft diagram of The Sci-Fi Collective. Start by reviewing the information you gathered on other relationships:

- A user can make multiple purchases. A purchase can be made by only one user.
- A user can maintain multiple payment methods. A payment method can be associated with only one user.
- [new] A payment method can be associated with multiple purchases. A purchase is associated with one payment method.
- A purchase can have more than one product. A product can show up in multiple purchases.

You can easily determine that the `product` and `purchase` relationship shouldn't fall into the one-to-many basket because if you examine its two directional relationships, neither has the max cardinality of one.

Similarly, it's not difficult to identify the `user` and `purchase` relationship as one-to-many because one of its two directional relationships has the max cardinality of one (from `purchase` to `user`) and the other has the max cardinality of many (from `user` to `purchase`). There is some ambiguity about the min cardinality from `user` to `purchase`, however, because a user can make multiple transactions. But what does *can* mean? After following up with the stakeholders, you learn that the relationship is optional. Think about when you browse an online store for an hour without buying anything. In other words, the min cardinality is zero. Update the `user` and `purchase` relationship as follows:

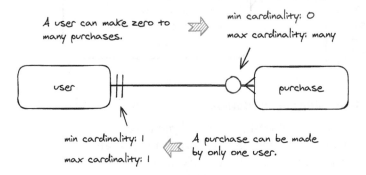

Next, insert a foreign key on the many side to establish this relationship fully:

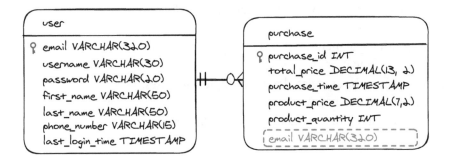

The relationships are one-to-many between `user` and `payment_ method` and between `purchase` and `payment_method`. Follow the same steps to update them:

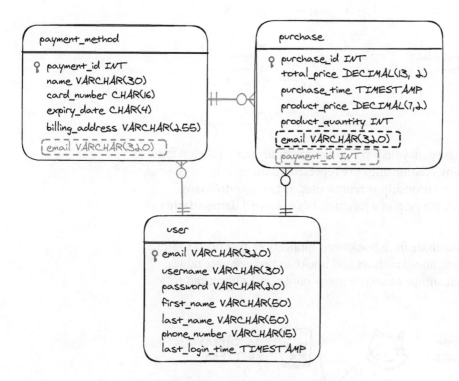

As you can see, you have two sets of relationships going from `payment_ method` to `user`; one set goes through the `purchase` entity, and the other is direct. This representation can lead to problems, which we will address in chapter 6.

Many-to-many: The more, the merrier

The last cardinality type you will learn is the many-to-many relationship. Like the other two types of relationships, many-to-many refers primarily to max cardinalities. If two entities are related, the max cardinality of both directional relationships is many, as shown in the following figure.

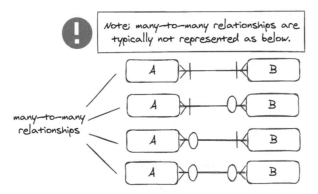

The preceding figure may help you grasp many-to-many relationships, but many-to-many relationships are represented differently. In general, a many-to-many relationship is represented as two one-to-many relationships with the help of a junction table, as we'll demonstrate in an example.

If you design a database for a bookstore application, you need to store all the information about authors and books in two separate tables. You know that an author can write many books and a book can have multiple authors.

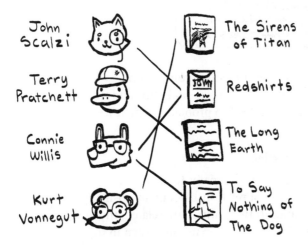

You know that this relationship is many-to-many as soon as you identify the max cardinalities of the two directional relationships:

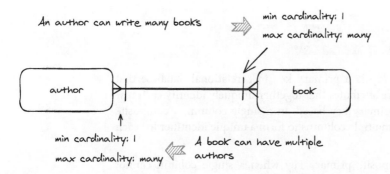

To represent this relationship properly, you need to go one step further by making a junction table that contains only the primary keys of the two involved entities: author and book. Also, you must convert the many-to-many relationship to two one-to-many relationships between the junction table and both entities. You can represent this many-to-many relationship as follows:

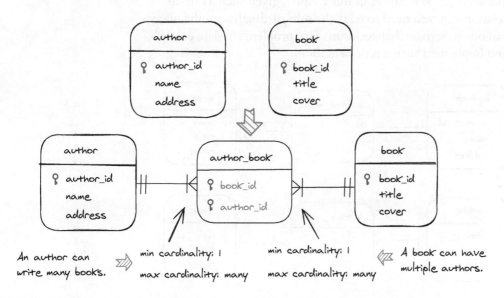

As you see, the junction table, author_book, contains only the primary keys from the author and book entities. In this junction table, the book_id and author_id attributes together serve as a composite primary key. It's worth noting that the crow's feet always point to the junction table. The author and book entities become indirectly related via the junction table.

Composite primary keys: The ultimate combination in databases

A *composite primary key* is a primary key in a relational database that consists of two or more attributes that together uniquely identify each row in a table. Unlike a primary key based on a single column, a composite primary key requires multiple columns to form a unique identifier for each record.

You must use a composite primary key when a single column cannot guarantee uniqueness for each row but a combination of multiple columns does. This type of key is commonly used when a table has a many-to-many relationship with another table or no simple key can uniquely identify a row in the table.

Now you have two one-to-many relationships whose min cardinalities are all ones. As you saw earlier in this chapter, given such a one-to-many relationship, you need to relax the min cardinality on the many side from one to zero so that you won't face problems in data entry when you implement such a representation.

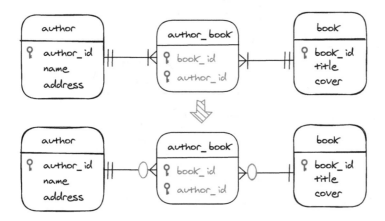

You may wonder why you can't simply insert a foreign key into both the entities in a many-to-many relationship. Well, representing a many-to-many relationship this way leads to data redundancy and difficulties in querying and modifying data. If you represent the `author` and `book` relationship this way, the data-redundancy problem jumps out immediately:

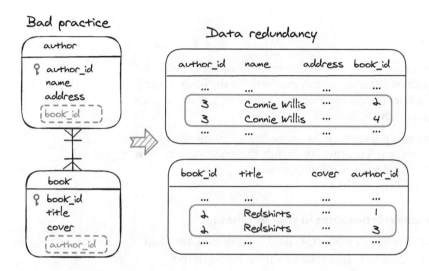

If an author wrote multiple books, the same author information has to occupy multiple rows in the author table even if they are redundant: different books have different book_id values, and book_id is the foreign key in the author table. Similarly, if a book has multiple authors, the information for the same book has to occupy multiple rows in the book table: different authors have different author_id values, and author_id is the foreign key in the book table. When the time comes to implement the two tables, having redundant primary key values, such as author_id in the author table, is impossible. Thus, simply inserting a foreign key into both tables involved in a many-to-many relationship is not viable.

Cardinality yoga: Learning to flex with zeros

The default min cardinality is often set to one. But you need to relax the min cardinalities from one to zero sometimes to enable data entry from time to time:

- In a one-to-one relationship, if one entity is typically created before the other, you might set the minimum cardinality of the second entity to zero to allow the first entity to exist without an immediate counterpart.

- In a one-to-many relationship, you can relax the cardinality that's closer to the many side to allow for cases in which the entity on the one side might exist without corresponding entries on the many side. A customer might exist without any addresses, for example.

(*continued*)

- In a many-to-many relationship, the minimum cardinalities are often set to zero on both sides if either entity can exist without the other. If there are strict business rules on the order of their existence, you might keep one of the two min cardinalities as one.

These rules of thumb may not always hold, depending on business rules and requirements, but you can still use them to identify three relationships with min cardinalities that require further examination.

Identify many-to-many relationships in your database

The draft diagram of The Sci-Fi Collective has one more relationship that you haven't worked on yet. This relationship is between the purchase and product entities:

> A purchase can have more than one product. A product can show up in multiple purchases.

After following up with the stakeholders for clarification, you see that a product doesn't necessarily need to show up in a purchase record, but a purchase record has to be associated with at least one product:

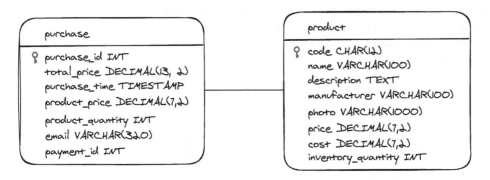

Based on this information, it is easy to identify this relationship as many-to-many and to determine the max and min cardinalities:

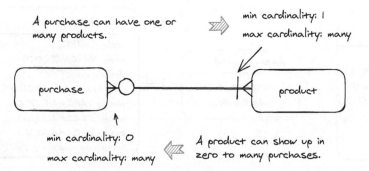

To represent this many-to-many relationship, make a junction table that contains only the primary keys from the purchase and product entities, and convert the many-to-many relationship to two one-to-many relationships:

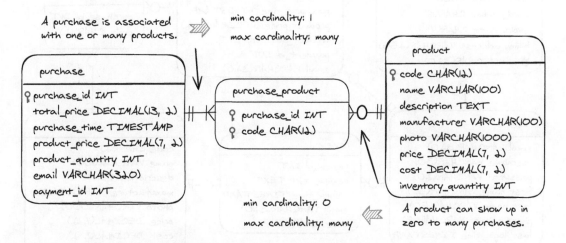

You may notice that the min cardinalities of the relationship between purchase and purchase_product are both one. To prevent problems with data entry when this representation is implemented, you should relax the min cardinality closer to the purchase_product side from one to zero, as shown in the following figure.

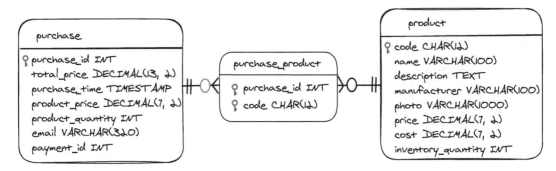

After all your updates to the draft E-R diagram, it looks like this:

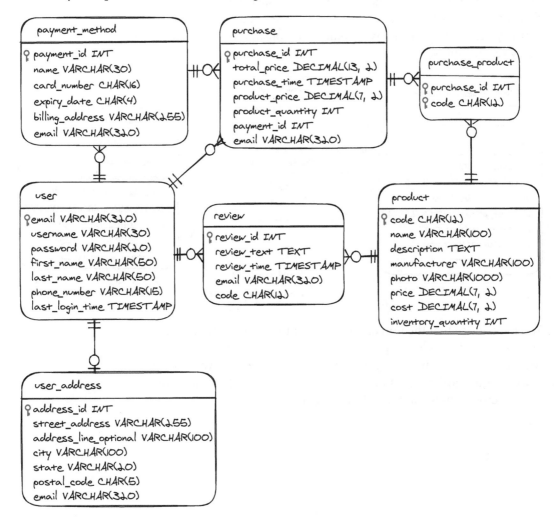

Strong and weak entities

Strong and weak entities are another characteristic of a relationship between two entities. This characteristic may come handy for refining E-R diagrams. In this section, you will learn about strong and weak entities and apply what you've learn to refine the E-R diagram of The Sci-Fi Collective.

At their core, *strong* and *weak entities* involve a dependency relationship between two entities. Given two related entities, if one is strong and the other is weak, the strong entity can exist on its own, but the weak entity cannot exist without the strong entity. In other words, weak entities cannot be uniquely identified by their attributes alone.

Let's try to understand strong and weak entities better via an example. Suppose that you are designing the database for a movie theater's web application and need to represent the relationship between movies (movie) and tickets (ticket). Between movie and ticket, movie is the strong entity because movie can exist independently in the database. By contrast, ticket is the weak entity because it depends on movie to identify each of its instances. The following figure depicts this relationship:

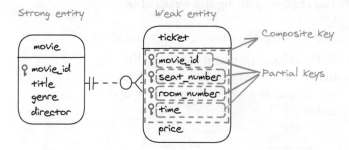

Typically, the primary key of the weak entity is a composite key that combines its own attribute(s) and the primary key of the related strong entity. As you see in the preceding figure, ticket uses a composite key composed of movie_id and other attributes. movie_id is the primary key in the movie entity, and the other attributes distinguish different tickets to the same movie. Such attributes are also known as *partial keys*.

It is worth noting, however, that strong and weak entities can always be converted to two strong entities. If tickets need to be managed independently for reselling and refund purposes, for example, you can convert `ticket` to a strong entity:

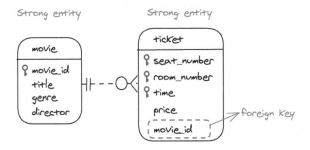

But what you should do if you have two entities that can be identified as both strong and weak? Should you identify them as strong and weak entities or treat them as two strong entities? The answer depends on a variety of factors, such as business demands, data representation and maintenance, and performance. If both options are possible, always choose the one that makes E-R diagrams simpler and less susceptible to bad data. As you apply this new knowledge to refine the E-R diagram of The Sci-Fi Collective further, you will see several examples that involve deciding whether to identify two entities as strong and weak entities.

Identify strong and weak entities in your database

In the E-R diagram of The Sci-Fi Collective, several entities fit the definition of weak entities, such as `review` and `payment_method`. You can see the `review` entity, for example, as a weak entity that depends on the existence of `user` and `product`:

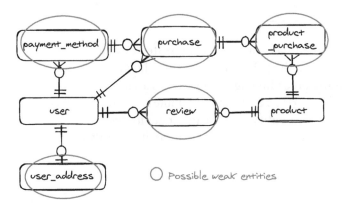

When you consider whether to convert a strong entity to a weak one, you should ask whether the decision will simplify the database design or improve data accuracy. If the answer is no, you should stay put. You could convert `review`, for example, to a weak entity that depends on `user` and `product`. But doing this means you need to start using a composite primary key in the `review` entity, which doesn't introduce any benefits but can lead to increased storage and slower query performance because composite primary keys require wider indexes and slower index lookup. As a result, you shouldn't convert `review` to a weak entity.

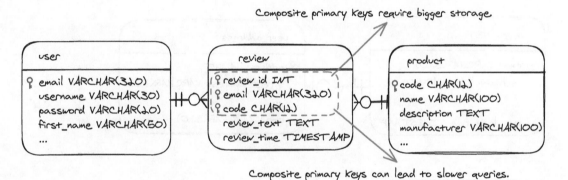

Composite primary keys require bigger storage.

Composite primary keys can lead to slower queries.

Following the same logic, you can tell that converting `payment_method` or `purchase` to weak entities is a bad idea. What about the `purchase_product` table? You can't change anything about `purchase_product` because it is already a weak entity. The `purchase_product` table is a junction table that you created to link `purchase` and `product` in a many-to-many relationship, and all junction tables are weak entities by nature. In this case, `purchase` and `product` are strong entities. As the weak entity, `purchase_product` uses a composite primary key composed of the primary keys of the two strong entities.

The `user_address` table turns out to be your only opportunity to apply your knowledge of strong and weak entities in refining the draft diagram. Your current design treats `user_address` as a strong entity that uses `address_id` as the primary key to identify each

of its instances and `email` as the foreign key to maintain the link
between `user_address` and `user`. If you convert `user_address` to
a weak entity, its primary key will become `email`, and the foreign
key will be gone. Why? The `user` and `user_address` entities are
in a one-to-one relationship, and `email` is good enough to identify
each instance of `user_address`. As a result, you no longer need
a composite primary key. Converting `user_address` to a weak
entity makes sense because it eliminates a foreign key constraint and
simplifies your design.

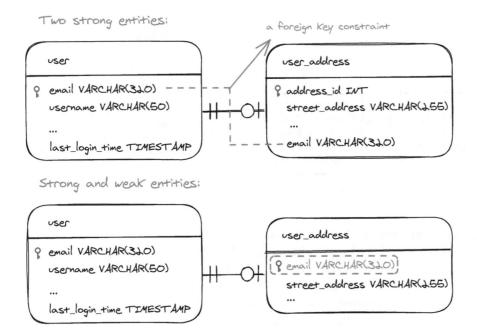

After you convert `user_address` to a weak entity, your E-R diagram
looks like this:

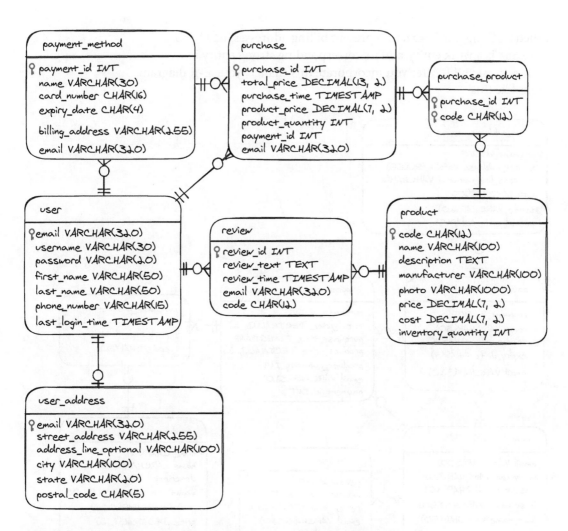

When you take a closer look at other tables and columns, you notice that `payment_method` contains a column, `billing_address`, that represents the billing address of a payment method. The relationship and nuances between a payment method and billing address are the same as between a user and user address. In other words, you need a table to fully represent the billing address the same way that you modeled `user_address`. Following the same logic, you can use a table called `billing_address` to represent billing addresses. `billing_address` is a weak entity, and its corresponding strong entity is `payment_method`. After you incorporate this change, your E-R diagram looks like this:

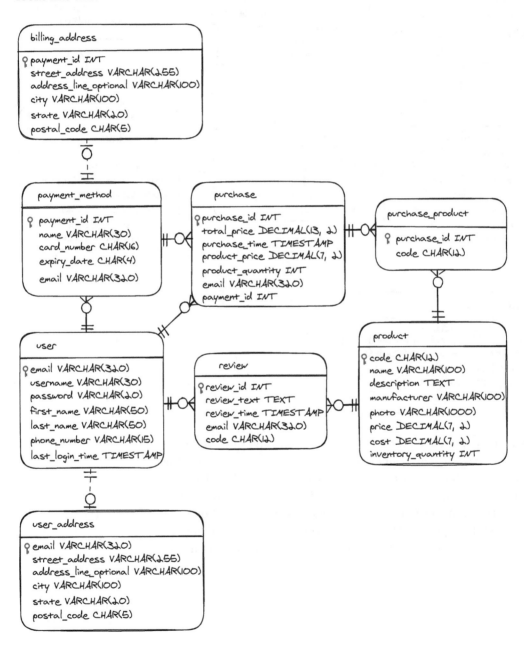

Give yourself a pat on the back: you have successfully wrapped up a round of data modeling by developing and refining your E-R diagram. Great job!

Recap

- Relationships are the binding glue between entities. The representations of relationships are informed by information from the requirements-gathering phase and further analysis.

- To represent relationships in an E-R diagram, you typically go through a three-step process: establishing relationships, identifying the cardinality of each relationship, and identifying potential weak entities and determining whether they should be converted to weak entities.

- Cardinality is an important characteristic of a relationship between two entities. Cardinalities come in three flavors: one-to-one, one-to-many, and many-to-many. Different flavors of cardinalities are represented differently, and the flavor has implications for where the foreign key is placed.

- In a one-to-one relationship, both the max cardinalities are one, represented by two bars. The foreign key connecting the two entities can be placed on either side.

- In a one-to-many relationship, the max cardinalities of the two directional relationships are one and many. Many is represented by the crow's foot. The foreign key should be placed on the many side indicated by the crow's foot.

- In a many-to-many relationship, both the max cardinalities of the two directional relationships are many. Representing a many-to-many relationship requires creating a junction table between the two entities and converting the relationship to two one-to-many relationships between each entity and the junction table. The junction table contains the primary keys of both entities.

- Strong and weak entities are another characteristic of a relationship. If two entities can be represented as strong and weak entities, you need to decide whether to do so, depending on whether such a representation makes the E-R diagram simpler and the database more efficient.

- A weak entity uses the primary key of its corresponding strong entity as part of its composite primary key. Other than that, a weak entity is not represented differently in Crow's Foot notation.

Normalization and implementation | 6

In this chapter

- You normalize your database design.

- You implement your database design.

- You learn important concepts such as using constraints and cascade.

What you need to know

You can find the database design covered in this chapter implemented in tools commonly used by practitioners, such as dbdiagram.io and MySQL Workbench, in the GitHub repository (https://github.com/Neo-Hao/grokking-relational-database-design). You can navigate to the `chapter_06` folder and follow the instructions in the `README.md` file to load the database design into corresponding tools.

You can also find the SQL scripts corresponding to the almost-finalized database design for different relational database management systems (RDBMSs), including MySQL, MariaDB, PostgreSQL, SQLite, SQL Server, and Oracle.

Overview

In this chapter, you will normalize and implement your database design for The Sci-Fi Collective. By doing so, you will learn about important concepts in database design, such as functional dependency, normalization, and constraints.

Normalization

Before converting your database design to a SQL script that creates the corresponding database and tables, you need to normalize your design. This critical step in database design is known as normalization.

Normalization is the process of organizing a database in a way that minimizes redundancy and dependency while maximizing data integrity and consistency. In other words, we break the database into smaller, more manageable tables, each table representing a single entity or concept. The primary goal of normalization is to strengthen data integrity. Although you have worked toward this goal in the preceding chapters, you are about to kick your work up a notch.

You will use normal forms to guide the normalization process. There are multiple normal forms, including the First Normal Form (1NF), Second Formal Form (2NF), Third Normal Form (3NF), and Boyce-Codd Normal Form (BCNF). The relationship among these normal forms is hierarchical and sequential in database normalization. Each form builds on the preceding one. Being the smallest nesting doll of these four normal forms, BCNF has all the characteristics of the other three.

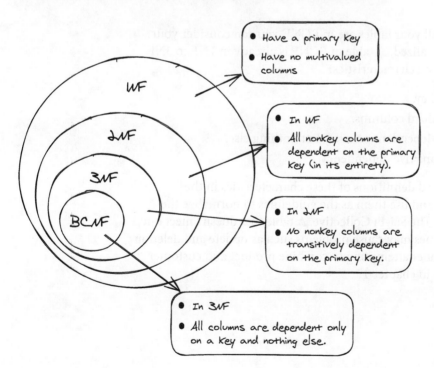

Superkeys, candidate keys, and primary keys

Do you remember what they are? The coverage of different types of keys goes back to chapter 4.

A *superkey* is a set of one or more columns of a table that can uniquely identify a row in the table, but it may contain columns that are not required to uniquely identify a row. A *candidate key* is a minimal superkey, which means that it is a superkey with no unnecessary columns. Of all the candidate keys in a table, one is chosen as the primary key. The following figure summarizes the relationships among the three types of key:

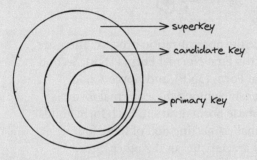

In practice, when all your tables are in BCNF, you can consider your database fully normalized. A table in BCNF is already in 1NF to 3NF and has the following characteristics:

- It has a primary key.
- It has no multivalued columns.
- All columns are dependent on a key but nothing else.
- It contains no transitive dependency.

You will find detailed definitions of these characteristics in the following sections and use them as the guidelines to normalize the database design of The Sci-Fi Collective. A table that doesn't meet one, two, or any guidelines may cause problems such as update and deletion anomalies. Remember attempting to combine product and customer data into one table in chapter 1?

product_id	name	price	manufacturer	customer_id	customer_name	customer_email	quantity
1	Atomic Nose ...	19.99	Mad Inventors Inc.	a1	Bob	bob@gmail.com	5
2	Selfie Toaster	24.99	Goofy Gadgets Corp.	b2	Dave	dave@outlook.com	15
3	Cat-Poop Coffee	29.99	Absurd Accessories	a1	Bob	bob@gmail.com	2
...	...	...	...	...	...	...	...
9	The Infinite ...	9.99	Silly Supplies Co.	j8	John	john@123.net	1
10	The Neuralyzer	33.55	Silly Supplies Co.	p9	Katy	katy@123.net	2

Normal forms: Crazy nesting dolls

You may wonder whether normal forms can go beyond BCNF. Yes! Fourth Normal Form (4NF), Fifth Normal Form (5NF), and even Sixth Normal Form (6NF) have been proposed and discussed in the theoretical framework of database normalization.

4NF, 5NF, and 6NF build on previous normal forms, and each form targets increasingly specific, less common design problems. 4NF addresses multivalued dependencies, for example, and 5NF eliminates redundancy caused by join dependencies that are not covered by 4NF. 6NF is largely theoretical.

4NF, 5NF, and 6NF are beyond the scope of this book. If you want a quick introduction to them, grab a textbook on databases (such as *Database System Concepts*, 7th ed., by A. Silberschatz, H. F. Korth, and S. Sudarshan [McGraw-Hill Education, 2019]) or make the following request of ChatGPT:

> Give me an introduction to 4NF, 5NF, and 6NF, using plain language and examples.

There is always a primary key

A table in BCNF should always have a primary key. Do you see primary keys everywhere in the entity-relationship (E-R) diagram you developed in chapter 5? Great! That means each table follows the first simple guideline of BCNF.

What if you have a table that doesn't have a primary key? Well, you need to stop and identify the primary key of that table before going any further.

There are no multivalued columns

A table in BCNF should have no multivalued columns. What is a multivalued column? Think about a table named `course_registration` that represents students taking a variety of courses. The `course` column is a multivalued column. Each course record holds multiple values.

The multivalued columns lead to problems such as difficult querying, data redundancy, inconsistency, and anomalies. You can easily spot a course repeated in different rows in `course_registration`, for example.

Who decides whether something is multivalued?

In a relational database, a table represents a single entity or a concept about which information is stored. A column in a table represents a specific attribute of the entity or concept that the table describes. Each column has a distinct name and a data type that defines the kind of data it stores. You may wonder who decides whether something should be considered a single concept, entity, or attribute. The answer is the users of the application supported by the database.

Determining whether a column is multivalued is based on the standards of users. In a table of an e-commerce database, for example, you would call out a column that represents phone numbers and stores multiple phone numbers per row as a multivalued column because each phone number represents a value that's undividable to users. Dividing a phone number into an area number and subscriber number makes no sense to any users of the database. As another example, you won't consider a column in the same database that stores single email addresses per row a multivalued column because users don't care about dividing an email address into a username and domain name.

Overall, user requirements decide the purposes of databases, which in turn decide whether a column is multivalued.

To fix such a problem, you typically need to redesign the multivalued column so that it holds only a single value in each row. Often, you need to move that multivalued column to a new table to prevent redundancy and other problems. To fix `course_registration`, for example, you limit the `course` column to hold a single course per row. But you can't repeat the same `student_id` values in different rows of the original table because it's the primary key. You need to break `course_registration` into two tables, one holding student information and the other holding course registration information:

🔑 student_id	student_name
124	Jacob Jeff
178	Brian Don
249	Tina Cloude

🔑 student_id	student_name	course
124	Jacob Jeff	Math, Biology, Physics
178	Brian Don	Biology, Computer science
249	Tina Cloude	Computer science, Math

🔑 student_id	course
124	Math
124	Biology
124	Physics
...	...
249	Math

Does your database design have you have any tables containing multivalued columns? Nope. When you mapped each entity to a table, you didn't attempt to use a column to hold more than one value. If you do, you will fix such problems in a similar manner.

All columns are dependent on a key but nothing else

All columns of a table in BCNF should be functionally dependent on a key. To understand this requirement, you need to understand functional dependency.

Think about how functions work in any programming language. Suppose that you have a function, `power(x)`, that takes `x` as the only input and returns its power as the output. Given the same input `x`, the function `power(x)` always returns the same output. The input functionally determines the output.

Now let's switch our attention to a table. In a table, given a value of column A, if there is always a unique corresponding value of column B, column A functionally determines column B—that is, column B is functionally dependent on column A. In the following table, which represents employees, `employee_name` is functionally dependent on `employee_id`. In other words, knowing the value of `employee_id` can help you determine the value of `employee_name`. This functional dependency can be expressed as follows:

```
employee_id → employee_name
```

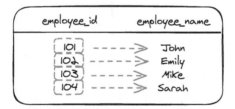

Functional dependency is directional. In the preceding figure, `employee_id` functionally determines `employee_name`. It doesn't mean, however, that `employee_name` functionally determines `employee_id`. The value of `employee_name` can't be used to determine the value of `employee_id`. Think what would happen if two different employees had the same name.

Now that you know what functional dependency is in the context of relational databases, look at this BCNF requirement again:

> A table in BCNF should have all its columns functionally dependent on a key but nothing else.

You may wonder why we say "dependent on a key" without specifying "primary key." There is a fine-grained difference, and edge cases exist. In most cases that you'll deal with in practice, however, you don't need to worry about it and can relax this requirement to the following:

> A table in BCNF should have all its columns functionally dependent on the primary key but nothing else.

Toward a deeper understanding of BCNF

A deep understanding of BCNF and all other normal forms is helpful in normalization (before they drive you crazy). Edge cases, which are good opportunities to deepen your understanding, are beyond the scope of this book, but it doesn't hurt to list them:

1. Table R has three columns, a, b, and c. The primary key of R is (a, b). If c is functionally dependent on a, R is not in 2NF, let alone 3NF or BCNF.

2. Table R has five columns, a, b, c, d, and e. The primary key of R is (a, b, c). d and e are functionally dependent on (a, b, c). If c is functionally dependent on d, R is in 3NF but not in BCNF.

3. Table R has five columns, a, b, c, d, and e. R has two candidate keys, (a, b) and (c, d). The primary key is (a, b). If e is functionally dependent only on (c, d), R is still in BCNF.

Before your head explodes, rest assured that you'll rarely need to deal with case 2 or 3.

In other words, if you find a table with one or more columns that are not functionally dependent on the primary key, the table must be normalized. How? You break the table into two or more tables, each table containing only the columns that are dependent on the primary. Depending on the relationship between the two new tables, you may link them via a foreign key.

We'll demonstrate this process with an example. Imagine a `product` table designed by a novice designer:

product_id	product_name	supplier_name	supplier_contact	category
1224	Stardust	Brewlux	555-0123	kitchen
3378	Time Machine	TimeCo	555-0456	utility
2549	Magic Wand	Magico	555-0789	utility

It may seem logical to include supplier contact information alongside product details for convenience. But the column `supplier_contact` is functionally dependent only on `supplier_name`. In other words, the `product` table contains two functional dependencies:

```
product_id → product_name, supplier_name, category
supplier_name → supplier_contact
```

To fix this problem, you need to remove the columns that are not determined by the primary key of the `product` table. Where do they fit in? A new table. The `supplier_contact` column is functionally dependent on `supplier_name`. If the two columns are in one table that represents suppliers, they fully meet the requirement of functional dependency. If each supplier can be identified by a unique ID, you can even use this piece of information as the primary key of this new table, and it will naturally become the foreign key in the `product` table that links `product` and `supplier`:

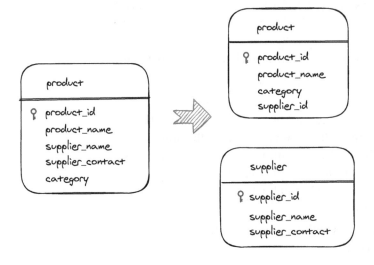

Normalize your database design

When you check the design of The Sci-Fi Collective's database against the requirement that all columns be functionally dependent on the primary key, you need to examine every table, including `purchase`:

```
purchase

⚷ purchase_id INT
   total_price DECIMAL(13, 2)
   purchase_time TIMESTAMP
   product_price DECIMAL(7, 2)
   product_quantity INT
   payment_id INT
```

Undoubtedly, many columns are functionally dependent on the primary key, including `total_price`, `purchase_time`, `payment_id`, and `email`. If you think about what goes into a receipt, you see that knowing the value of `purchase_id` is equal to having a receipt, which determines the values of `total_price` and `purchase_time`:

```
        The Sci-Fi Collective
         Receipt of Purchase
       2023-01-01 00:00:00
            # 311205

                         Quantities   Price
Atomic Nose Hair Trimmer      1          5
Selfie Toaster                2          3
Cat-Poop Coffee               3          2
Inflatable Briefcase          3          2

                          Total:       12
```

From this example receipt, you can tell that each purchase involves multiple products with different quantities and prices. Product quantities (`product_quantity`) and prices (`product_price`) are functionally determined by a combination of purchase ID (`purchase_id`) and product code (`code`). The product code (`code`) isn't in the `purchase` table. That said, you have two functional dependencies in this table:

```
product_id → total_price, purchase_time, payment_id, email
purchase_id, code → product_quantity, product_price
```

Because of the two functional dependencies, this table violates BCNF.

When you start adding data to the `purchase` table, you see how tricky the problem is. Adding the data of a receipt to the `purchase` table, for example, is a mission impossible:

You can't repeat the values of the primary key. Even if you could, you would still face redundancy problems in other columns, such as `total_price` and `purchase_time`.

To fix this problem, move the columns that are not functionally dependent on the primary key to a new table. In this case, `product_quantity` and `product_price` are functionally dependent on the combination of `purchase_id` and `code`. But neither `purchase_id` nor `code` can functionally determine `product_quantity` or `product_price` alone:

- `purchase_id` does not functionally determine `product_quantity` or `product_price`. Each purchase can include multiple products with different quantities and prices.

- `code` does not functionally determine `product_quantity` or `product_price` in the context of a purchase. The same product can be sold in different quantities and at different prices in various purchases.

Luckily, you already have a junction table, `purchase_product`, that connects `purchase` and `product`. The junction table uses the combo of `purchase_id` and `code` as its primary key. Moving `product_quantity` and `product_price` to the `purchase_product` table is like killing two birds with one stone. With this change, both `purchase` and `purchase_product` meet the requirement of functional dependency:

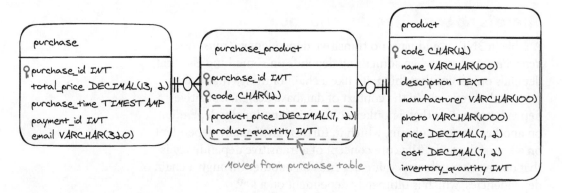

Moved from purchase table

You may be tempted to eliminate `product_price` from the `purchase_product` table because you can always retrieve a product's price from the `product` table. But it's best not to do that. Over time, the price of a product may change due to factors such as inflation or market competition. If you rely on only the `product` table to retrieve product prices, you may lose the data required to put together a receipt from several months ago. For the same reason, you should add a product name column to the `purchase_product` table. After all, nothing should lead to changes in a receipt—not even product name changes.

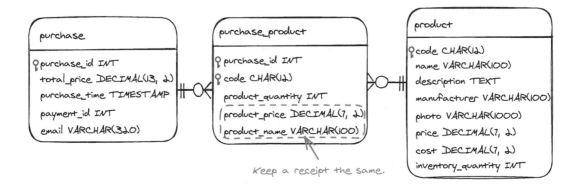

Keep a receipt the same.

There is no transitive dependency

A table in 3NF should have no transitive dependency. *Transitive dependency* occurs when something depends on something else that depends on yet another thing; it's like a chain of things that need one another to work. In the context of database design, transitive dependency means that a nonkey column is functionally dependent on another nonkey column, which in turn is functionally dependent on a key of the table. The core concept of a transitive dependency is that one nonkey column's value depends on another through a chain of dependencies, which is ultimately dependent on a key.

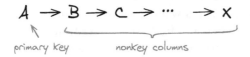

A table representing employees has the following columns and functional dependencies:

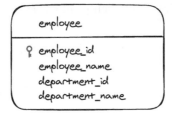

employee_id → department_id → department_name

The primary key of the `employee` table is `employee_id`. In this table, `department_name` is dependent on `department_id`, and `department_id` is dependent on `employee_id`. This chained functional dependency is transitive dependency.

Transitive dependency is problematic. If a table contains transitive dependency, it leads to all kinds of problems, such as data redundancy and insertion/update/deletion anomalies. Updating a department name in the preceding `employee table` properly means updating all the `department_name` values in every row:

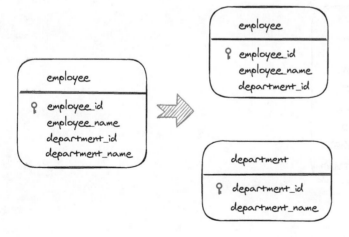

What should you do with a table containing transitive dependency? Break the table into two or more tables, each table containing columns that are directly dependent on a key and dependent only on that key. Depending on the relationship between the two new tables, you may link them via a foreign key. If you stick to this principle, break the `employee` table into two tables as follows:

The `department` table contains the nonkey columns that are involved in the transitive dependency, with the `department_id` as its primary key. The new `employee` table contains only the columns that are directly dependent on `employee_id` and dependent only on it, including the foreign key `department_id`. A foreign key is always directly dependent on the primary key because each row has a unique combination of the primary key and foreign key.

Normalize your database design: A cycle involving three tables

A transitive dependency may be hard to spot without a deep understanding of the data, requirement analysis, and some sample data. Your `purchase` table, for example, uses two foreign keys, `email` and `payment_id`, to maintain its relationships with the `payment_method` and `user` tables:

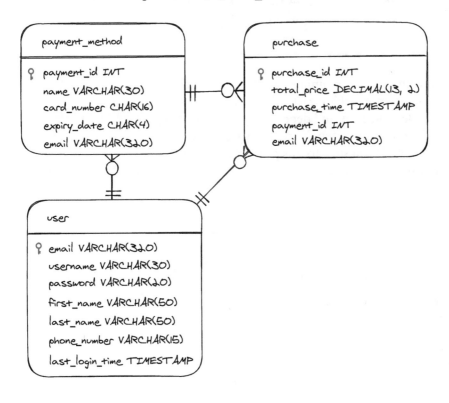

Without question, in the purchase table, all other non-primary-key columns are dependent on the primary key, including the foreign keys.

If you look beyond the purchase table, however, you notice something unexpected: the two foreign keys in the purchase table, payment_id and email, have a dependency relationship. From the payment_method table, you see that email is a foreign key that helps maintain the relationship between payment_method and user. As in the purchase table, the foreign key (email) is dependent on the primary key (payment_method). When you consider this new piece of information, you see a transitive dependency in purchase:

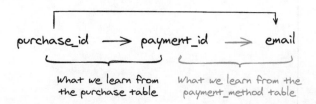

In theory, you need only two relationships to connect three tables. If you notice that you are using three relationships and that the relationships are starting to look like a cycle in your E-R diagram, you may have a transitive dependency somewhere.

Now that you have identified the transitive dependency, how do you fix it? The principle is the same a table should contain only columns that are directly dependent on the primary key and dependent only on it. You can remove the email column from the purchase table to break the direct relationship between the user and purchase tables, but user is still related to purchase via payment_method, as shown in the following figure.

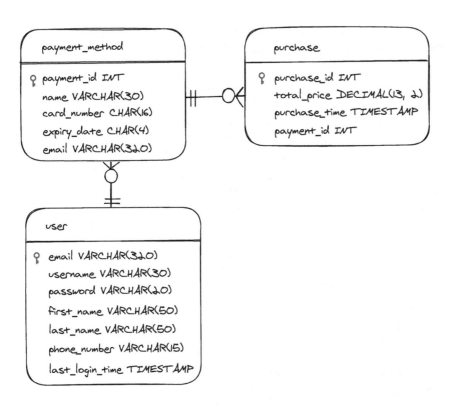

If normalization is your only concern, removing the link between the user and purchase tables is a brilliant move. But it may not be the best move if you are also concerned with other problems, such as query speed and cost. We will revisit the relationship between the user and purchase tables in chapter 7.

When you go through all other tables in your database design, you won't see other transitive dependency problems. That said, you have completed all the steps to check each table against the 3NF requirements:

- It has a primary key.
- It has no multivalued columns.
- All columns are dependent on a key but nothing else.
- It contains no transitive dependency. (All its nonkey columns are directly dependent on a key.)

Your updated E-R diagram looks like this:

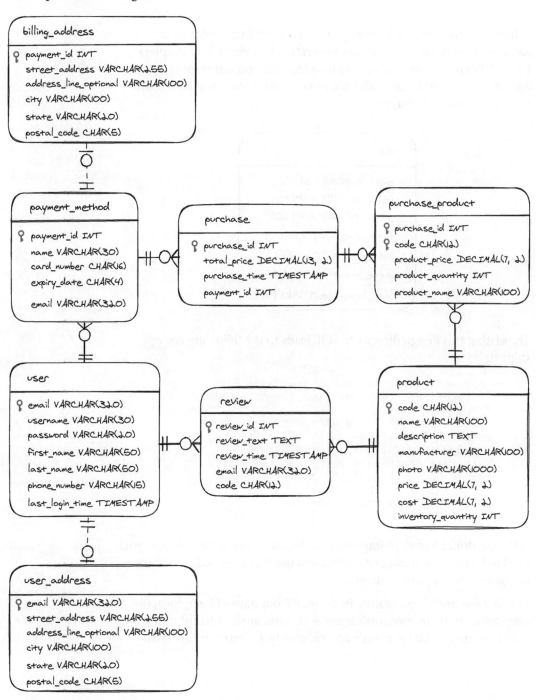

Implementation

When you finish normalization, you are ready to implement your database design. You learned how to create tables via SQL in chapters 1 and 2. With this knowledge, you may feel that you can translate your database design into SQL with little to no effort. Your `user` table looks like this in your E-R diagram:

Translating this design directly to SQL leads to the following code snippet:

```
-- comment: works for MySQL and MariaDB
-- comment: see the code repo for other RDBMS
CREATE TABLE user (
   email VARCHAR(320) PRIMARY KEY,
   username VARCHAR(30),
   password VARCHAR(20),
   first_name VARCHAR(50),
   last_name VARCHAR(50),
   phone_number VARCHAR(15),
   last_login_time TIMESTAMP
);
```

Is the job done? Nope. To implement a database design successfully, you need to learn more about constraints and use that knowledge to make decisions beyond the E-R diagram.

You saw the use of constraints in chapter 2 but haven't been formally introduced to them. *Constraints* are SQL rules applied to columns in a table to ensure data accuracy and reliability. Constraints are used to enforce data integrity and can be established during or after table creation. Are you worried that software developers may not follow your database design when they develop the APIs? When you apply constraints to your tables, they have to listen! Without constraints, a database is like a toddler on a sugar high: chaotic and prone to causing havoc.

In the following sections, you learn about common SQL constraints and other design decisions that you need to make. We don't strive to cover all the constraints or SQL code required to implement the database. If you want to see the full SQL script, refer to the GitHub repository (https://mng.bz/4ao5).

NOT NULL: Can't have null-thing to say

The NOT NULL constraint ensures that a column does not accept NULL values in SQL. In other words, when the NOT NULL constraint is applied to a column, you have to provide a value for that column. The NOT NULL constraint can be handy for preventing problems in data storage and analytics. As we stated in chapter 1, a NULL value in SQL represents an unknown value. Allowing NULL values for columns may lead to unexpected behaviors in SQL.

When do you need help from NOT NULL constraints? In most cases. Although their use depends on the requirements and the data, NOT NULL constraints are commonly applied in a wide range of scenarios. Columns that contain critical information for business operations (such as usernames, email addresses, or passwords) often have NOT NULL constraints. As another example, legal or compliance reasons force some columns to use NOT NULL constraints, such as date of birth in an option-trading application. Also, when two tables are related, the foreign keys may need NOT NULL constraints, depending on the nature of the relationship. You learn more about how NOT NULL constraints are used with foreign keys later in this chapter.

Do you have any columns that require NOT NULL constraints in the database design of The Sci-Fi Collective? Yes. Many columns in your database design contain critical data necessary for business operations. Six columns in the user table fall into this basket: username, email, password, first_name, last_name, and last_login_time.

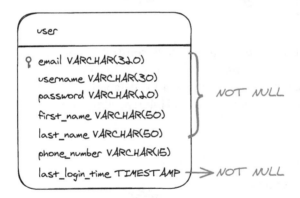

As a result, you'll add NOT NULL constrains to these columns. You can do so by adding NOT NULL in the same code lines that define columns:

```
-- comment: works for MySQL, MariaDB, and SQLite
-- comment: see the code repo for other RDBMS
CREATE TABLE user (
   email VARCHAR(320) PRIMARY KEY,
   username VARCHAR(30) NOT NULL,
   password VARCHAR(20) NOT NULL,
   first_name VARCHAR(50) NOT NULL,
   last_name VARCHAR(50) NOT NULL,
   phone_number VARCHAR(15),
   last_login_time TIMESTAMP NOT NULL
);
```

You may notice that the primary key, `email`, doesn't have the NOT NULL constraint. The reason is that it already has the PRIMARY KEY constraint, which implies a NOT NULL constraint and enforces it automatically. You learn more about the PRIMARY KEY constraint in the following section.

Primary key: The one and only

As you already know, in a solid database design, every table has a primary key. When such a design is translated to SQL, it is expressed as the primary key constraint.

The primary key constraint ensures that no duplicate rows with the same primary key exist in the same table. In addition, the primary key constraint guarantees that no row with a NULL value in the primary key column can be inserted into the table.

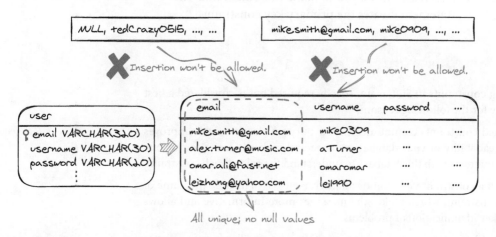

The syntax of a primary key constraint is simple. You can add PRIMARY KEY to the code line that defines the column:

```
-- comment: works for MySQL, MariaDB and PostgreSQL
-- comment: see the code repo for other RDBMS
CREATE TABLE user (
  email VARCHAR(320) PRIMARY KEY,
  username VARCHAR(30) NOT NULL,
  password VARCHAR(20) NOT NULL,
  first_name VARCHAR(50) NOT NULL,
  last_name VARCHAR(50) NOT NULL,
  phone_number VARCHAR(15),
  last_login_time TIMESTAMP NOT NULL
);
```

If your database design is ongoing and there's a chance that the primary key may change, however, you want to name the primary key constraint explicitly:

```
-- comment: works for MySQL, MariaDB and PostgreSQL
-- comment: see the code repo for other RDBMS
CREATE TABLE user (
  email VARCHAR(320),
  username VARCHAR(30) NOT NULL,
  password VARCHAR(20) NOT NULL,
  first_name VARCHAR(50) NOT NULL,
  last_name VARCHAR(50) NOT NULL,
  phone_number VARCHAR(15),
  last_login_time TIMESTAMP NOT NULL,
  CONSTRAINT pk_user PRIMARY KEY (email)
);
```

The CONSTRAINT... clause allows you to name this constraint. The PRIMARY KEY... statement creates the primary key constraint.

Naming constraints: A best practice

Naming constraints in SQL is not strictly required but is considered a best practice for the following reasons:

- Named constraints communicate their purpose clearly, which improves the readability of your database schema and makes it easier for anyone who interacts with the database to understand the role of each constraint.

- When a constraint violation occurs, error messages include the name of the constraint, which makes the messages more informative and allows quicker identification of problems.

- If you don't name a constraint, the SQL system will generate a name automatically. Autogenerated names are often meaningless and vary from one RDBMS to another, which may lead to confusion, especially when you're porting the database schema to a different system.

Certain constraints, such as NOT NULL and DEFAULT, are not always named. These constraints usually are integral parts of column definitions and could rarely be referenced separately; keeping them as part of column definition may make SQL scripts easier to write and simpler to read. In the case of other constraints, such as primary key and foreign key, if there is even a small chance that you'll need to restructure or migrate the database, you had better keep them named.

What if you have a composite primary key that is composed of more than one column? You can define the primary key separately from any individual column definition. In the E-R diagram of The Sci-Fi Collective, the `purchase_product` table uses a composite primary key composed of two columns, `purchase_id` and `code`. You can define this primary key separately from individual column definitions as follows:

```
-- comment: works for MySQL, MariaDB, and PostgreSQL
-- comment: see the code repo for other RDBMS
CREATE TABLE purchase_product (
  purchase_id INT NOT NULL,
  code CHAR(12) NOT NULL,
  product_price DECIMAL(7,2) NOT NULL,
  product_quantity INT NOT NULL,
  product_name VARCHAR(100) NOT NULL,
  CONSTRAINT pk_purchase_product
    PRIMARY KEY (purchase_id, code)
);
```

Foreign key: Playing Cupid

When two tables have a relationship, you use a foreign key to link them. As you know, a *foreign key* is at least one column in a table that refers to the primary key in another table. When a foreign key is translated to SQL, it is typically expressed as the foreign key constraint.

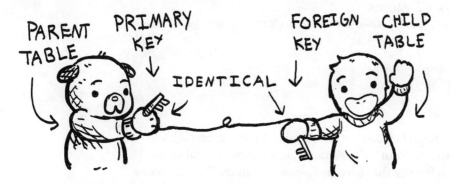

The foreign key constraint enforces referential integrity. What is referential integrity? Given a relationship between two tables, one table contains the foreign key that references the primary key of the other table. From chapter 2, you know that the table containing the foreign key is called a *child table*, and the other table is called a *parent table*. If you attempt to add a row to the child table but your foreign key value doesn't exist yet in the parent table, SQL would stop you and complain.

You have a one-to-many relationship between the user and review tables in the E-R diagram of The Sci-Fi Collective, for example. In the review table, email is the foreign key that links review to user. If the foreign key constraint is implemented properly, SQL should stop you if you try to add a review record with an email value that doesn't exist in user yet.

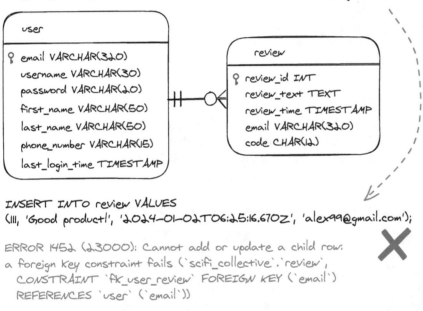

Note: user table doesn't contain an email value as alex99@gmail.com.

```
INSERT INTO review VALUES
(111, 'Good product!', '2024-01-02T06:25:16.670Z', 'alex99@gmail.com');
```

ERROR 1452 (23000): Cannot add or update a child row:
a foreign key constraint fails (`scifi_collective`.`review`,
CONSTRAINT `fk_user_review` FOREIGN KEY (`email`)
REFERENCES `user` (`email`))

Implementing a foreign key constraint is similar to implementing a primary key constraint. Your review table, for example, contains two foreign keys that reference the user and product tables. You can define and name the foreign key constraints when creating the review table:

```
-- comment: works for MySQL and MariaDB
-- comment: see the code repo for other RDBMS
CREATE TABLE review (
    review_id INT PRIMARY KEY,
    review_text TEXT NOT NULL,
```

```
  review_time TIMESTAMP NOT NULL,
  email VARCHAR(320) NOT NULL,
  code CHAR(12) NOT NULL,
  CONSTRAINT fk_user_review
    FOREIGN KEY (email) REFERENCES user(email),
  CONSTRAINT fk_product_review
    FOREIGN KEY (code) REFERENCES product(code)
);
```

Or you can define the foreign key constraints after the review table is created:

```
-- comment: works for MySQL, MariaDB and PostgreSQL
-- comment: SQLite doesn't support
-- comment: ALTER TABLE ADD CONSTRAINT
-- step 1: create the review table first
CREATE TABLE review (
  review_id INT PRIMARY KEY,
  review_text TEXT NOT NULL,
  review_time TIMESTAMP NOT NULL,
  email VARCHAR(320) NOT NULL,
  code CHAR(12) NOT NULL
);
-- step 2: add foreign key constraints afterward
ALTER TABLE review
  ADD CONSTRAINT fk_user_review
    FOREIGN KEY (email) REFERENCES user(email),
  ADD CONSTRAINT fk_product_review
    FOREIGN KEY (code) REFERENCES product(code)
```

In the same way that a primary key constraint is defined and named, the CONSTRAINT... clause names a constraint, and the FOREIGN KEY... REFERENCES... statement creates a foreign key constraint that enforces referential integrity.

It is worth noting that when a relationship is mandatory, the foreign key typically requires help from the NOT NULL constraint. When the minimum cardinality of a directional relationship is one, that directional relationship is considered mandatory. The relationship from review to user in your database design, for example, is mandatory: the min cardinality is one, which means that a review is associated with at least one user. If you have a review record that doesn't reference any users in the user table, this row can't be added to the review table. That said, allowing email in review to accept NULL values makes no sense because a NULL value of email doesn't reference any users.

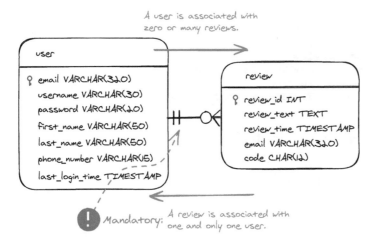

Referential actions

In the preceding section, you learned that you can use foreign key constraints to enforce one aspect of referential integrity: data insertion. When someone tries to insert a row into a child table, but the foreign key value in that row doesn't reference anything in the parent table, the foreign key constraint will stop the operation and raise a complaint.

Beyond data insertion, referential integrity cares about data deletion and updating. When a row is removed from the parent table, how should the corresponding rows in the child be handled? When a row's primary key value is updated in the parent table, what should happen to the corresponding rows in the child table?

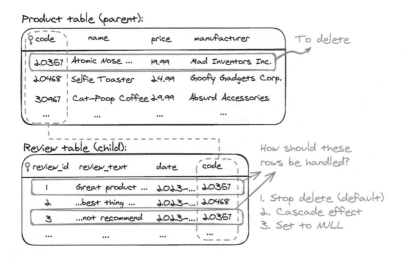

You can handle such problems by respecting the default action, which prevents you from updating or deleting a row in the parent table if there are matching rows in the child table. To respect the default actions, either do nothing or expand the foreign key constraint definitions with the following statements:

```
ON DELETE RESTRICT
ON UPDATE RESTRICT
```

The ON DELETE line defines how to handle the corresponding rows in the child table when a row is deleted in the parent table. The ON UPDATE line defines how to handle the corresponding rows in the child table when a row's primary key is updated in the parent table. You can also swap RESTRICT with NO ACTION, which has the same effect. These clauses are known as *referential actions*, which are triggered automatically when you update primary key values or delete rows in the parent table.

The default action, RESTRICT (or NO ACTION) maintains the integrity and consistency of the database by preventing you from deleting or updating a parent table. But what if you need to delete some data or update a primary key value in a parent table? To maintain the integrity and consistency of the database, use a different type of referential action, called CASCADE:

- CASCADE *delete*—If a row in the parent table is deleted, the corresponding rows in the child table are automatically be deleted if possible. This action ensures that no rows in the child table lack corresponding rows in the parent table.
- CASCADE *update*—If a primary key in the parent table changes, the corresponding foreign keys in the child table automatically update with the new key value. This action ensures that the link between the two tables is maintained without manual update operations.

The implementation of a CASCADE action is simple. You expand your foreign key constraint definitions a bit to include two different statements:

```
ON DELETE CASCADE
ON UPDATE CASCADE
```

You see the CASCADE effect in the child table whenever a row is deleted or a row's primary key is updated in the parent table.

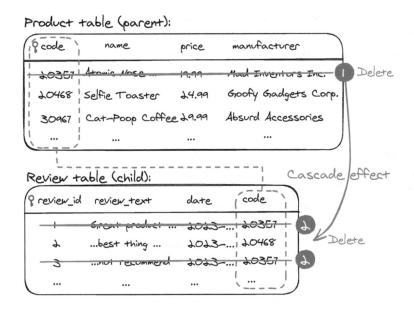

Product table (parent):

Review table (child):

In a less common scenario, you may want to support the delete operation in the parent table but preserve the corresponding rows in the child table. A database that tracks company assets might have two related tables, `device` and `employee`. If an employee leaves the company and is removed from `employee`, it may be beneficial to retain the corresponding rows in `device` because those devices still exist in the company's inventory. In such a scenario, you can use the help of another type of referential action, SET NULL:

```
ON DELETE SET NULL
ON UPDATE CASCADE
```

With the help of SET NULL, all corresponding foreign keys in the child table are converted to NULL, and data in other columns is retained when a row is deleted in the parent table. The SET NULL action can be handy when a relationship between two tables is nonessential or when you need to retain the child rows for recordkeeping. But this action may introduce problems, such as creating orphan rows or complicating queries that expect non-null foreign keys down the road.

Do you have any relationships that need help from explicit referential actions in the database design of The Sci-Fi Collective? Yes. The `user` table, for example, is a parent table of other tables, including `payment_method`. The `email` column is the primary key of the `user` table.

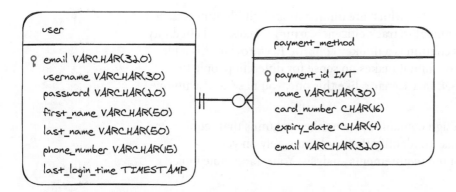

If The Sci-Fi Collective ever allows users to change their email addresses or delete their accounts, many possible updates and deletions may occur in the parent table. To maintain the integrity and consistency of the database, you can opt for the CASCADE action, which is part of the foreign key constraint in the payment_method table:

```
-- comment: works for MySQL, MariaDB and PostgreSQL
-- comment: see the code repo for other RDBMS
CREATE TABLE payment_method (
  payment_id INT PRIMARY KEY,
  name VARCHAR(30) NOT NULL,
  card_number CHAR(16) NOT NULL,
  expiry_date CHAR(4) NOT NULL,
  email VARCHAR(320) NOT NULL,
  CONSTRAINT fk_payment_method_user
    FOREIGN KEY (email) REFERENCES user (email)
    ON DELETE CASCADE
    ON UPDATE CASCADE
);
```

Unique: Sorry, I'm taken

Unique constraints ensure that all values in a column or a combination of columns are different. If you have some nonkey columns that should all contain unique values, you need to apply unique constraints.

You need unique constraints when you have a single column or a combination of nonkey columns for which duplicate values make no sense in the real world. Consider a table containing a column that represents Social

Security numbers (SSN), which are unique nine-digit identifiers issued by the U.S. government to track citizens' earnings, taxes, and eligibility for benefits. This column is a nonkey column. Each row in this table represents a person, and it makes no sense for different people to have the same SSN. In a scenario like this one, you need to use unique constraints.

Your database design contains some nonkey columns that require unique constraints. To identify these columns, rely on your understanding of the requirements analysis. Your `user` table looks like this:

The requirements analysis tells you that both the `username` and `phone_number` columns need to hold unique values. Both columns are be nonkey columns. As a result, you should add unique constraints to these two columns and name them accordingly:

```
-- comment: works for MySQL, MariaDB and PostgreSQL
-- comment: see the code repo for other RDBMS
CREATE TABLE user (
  email VARCHAR(320) PRIMARY KEY,
  username VARCHAR(30) NOT NULL,
  password VARCHAR(20) NOT NULL,
  first_name VARCHAR(50) NOT NULL,
  last_name VARCHAR(50) NOT NULL,
  phone_number VARCHAR(15),
  last_login_name TIMESTAMP NOT NULL,
  CONSTRAINT unq_username UNIQUE (username),
  CONSTRAINT unq_phone_number UNIQUE (phone_number)
);
```

Sometimes, you need to apply the unique constraint to a combination of columns. Consider your `product` table:

If your requirements analysis says you need to ensure the uniqueness of the combination of two pieces of information, the name and manufacturer of a product, you need to apply the unique constraint to a combination of the two columns:

```
-- comment: works for MySQL, MariaDB and PostgreSQL
-- comment: see the code repo for other RDBMS
CREATE TABLE product (
   code CHAR(12) PRIMARY KEY,
   name VARCHAR(100) NOT NULL,
   description TEXT NOT NULL,
   manufacturer VARCHAR(100) NOT NULL,
   photo VARCHAR(1000) NOT NULL,
   price DECIMAL(7,2) NOT NULL,
   cost DECIMAL(7,2) NOT NULL,
   inventory_quantity INT,
   CONSTRAINT unq_name_manufacturer
      UNIQUE(name, manufacturer)
);
```

Default to awesome

You use the default constraint to set a default value for a column when a new row is inserted into the table and no value is provided for that column. The default constraint ensures that a column always has a value, specified by either the user or the constraint.

You typically use the default constraint in the following situations:

- You have a column that stores timestamps, such as a column representing when a row is created or modified.
- You have a numeric column on which you might perform aggregation, such as a column representing the quantity or price.
- You have a column that is optional and can use the help of a placeholder value.

Your database design has columns that could use default constraints. Your `purchase` table, for example, has a `purchase_time` column that stores timestamps:

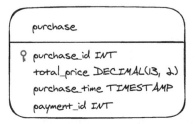

When a purchase is made online, a row of data is supposed to be inserted into the `purchase` table. Instead of relying solely on the software developers to do the right thing, you can lessen their burden by setting the default value of `purchase_time` to the time when a row of purchase data is added. The syntax of the default constraint is simple. Add the `DEFAULT` value to the same line of your column definition, and make sure to provide the proper target value:

```
CREATE TABLE purchase (
   purchase_id INT PRIMARY KEY,
   total_price DECIMAL(13,2) NOT NULL,
   purchase_time TIMESTAMP NOT NULL
   DEFAULT CURRENT_TIMESTAMP,
   payment_id INT NOT NULL,
   CONSTRAINT fk_payment_method_purchase
      FOREIGN KEY (payment_id)
      REFERENCES payment_method(payment_id)
);
```

Two things in the preceding SQL snippet require explanation:

- Both `NOT NULL` and default constraints were added to the `purchase_time` column. You may wonder whether the `NOT NULL` constraint is still necessary, considering that the default value is already set. Well, it is useful, especially if `NULL` values are problematic for that column. The default constraint, after all, doesn't prevent users from adding `NULL` values.

- The default value was set to `CURRENT_TIMESTAMP`, which is a widely supported function in most RDBMSs, including MySQL, MariaDB, SQLite, and PostgreSQL. `CURRENT_TIMESTAMP` is commonly used to obtain the current date and time.

Clocking databases: Navigating UTC across RDBMSs

In chapter 4, we recommended storing date and time values in Coordinated Universal Time (UTC) because UTC ensures consistency and prevents problems such as Daylight Saving Time changes and different time zones.

Does CURRENT_TIMESTAMP adopt UTC automatically? The answer depends on the RDBMS you use. CURRENT_TIMESTAMP achieves what you want in MySQL, for example, because the temporal data in MySQL is stored in UTC by default. By contrast, TIMESTAMP comes in two flavors in PostgreSQL. To get what you want in PostgreSQL, you need to specify the data type of purchase_time as TIMESTAMP WITH TIME ZONE. When you do, CURRENT_TIMESTAMP automatically stores temporal data in UTC:

```
-- PostgreSQL
CREATE TABLE purchase (
  purchase_id INT PRIMARY KEY,
  total_price DECIMAL(13,2) NOT NULL,
  purchase_time TIMESTAMP
      WITH TIME ZONE NOT NULL
      DEFAULT CURRENT_TIMESTAMP,
  payment_id INT NOT NULL,
  CONSTRAINT fk_payment_method_purchase
      FOREIGN KEY (payment_id)
          REFERENCES payment_method(payment_id)
);
```

The TIMESTAMP data types also come in two flavors in PostgreSQL:

- TIMESTAMP WITHOUT TIME ZONE (TIMESTAMP is the same)

- TIMESTAMP WITH TIME ZONE

To enable time zones, you declare the data type of the target column as TIMESTAMP WITH TIME ZONE. Otherwise, the data that you store in that column will carry no time-zone information. This is one thing you want to double-check in the manual of the RDBMS that you use. Or ask ChatGPT when you're about to use some RDBMS that's new to you:

- How do I create a column representing the current time and store data in that column in UTC in SQLite?

- How do I create a column representing the current time and store data in that column in UTC in SQL Server?

Check: Enforce data decorum

A *check constraint* is a rule that specifies a condition each row must meet for the data to be considered valid in a column. You can use a check constraint to enforce data integrity by restricting the values that can be inserted into columns.

You need a check constraint when you want to enforce specific rules on the data, such as enforcing data ranges or validating data formats. If you have a column representing the ages of people, for example, you can use a check constraint to limit the table to accept only values between 0 and 120:

```
-- comment: works for MySQL, MariaDB and PostgreSQL
CREATE TABLE person (
  person_id int NOT NULL,
  last_name varchar(255) NOT NULL,
  first_name varchar(255),
  age int,
  CONSTRAINT age_check CHECK (age >= 0 AND age <= 120)
);
```

In the preceding example, `Age >= 0 AND Age <= 120` is the condition of the check constraint.

Do you have any columns that can use check constraints in your database design? You have one case that fits the preceding scenarios perfectly. Both your `user_address` and `billing_address` tables contain a `state column` that stores the names of states in the United States. The valid values of this column are limited to 50 known names. Instead of relying on your frontend or backend developers to do the right thing, you can use the check constraint to take the burden off their shoulders. Given that 50 is not a small number, you can opt to add the constraint after you create the table, as follows:

```
-- comment: works for MySQL, MariaDB, PostgreSQL, and
-- comment: Oracle; see the code repo for other RDBMS
CREATE TABLE user_address (
  email VARCHAR(320) PRIMARY KEY,
  street_address VARCHAR(255),
  address_line_optional VARCHAR(100),
  city CHAR(100) NOT NULL,
  state VARCHAR(20) NOT NULL,
  postal_code CHAR(5) NOT NULL
);
```

```
ALTER TABLE user_address
 ADD CONSTRAINT chk_state
 CHECK (
  state IN (
   'Alabama', 'Alaska', 'Arizona',
   'Arkansas', 'California', ...,
   'West Virginia', 'Wisconsin', 'Wyoming'
  )
);
```

(`'Alabama'`, `'Alaska'`, … `'Wyoming'`) defines a list of the allowed values. The `IN` keyword requires all the values in that column to be one of the values in the list.

Recap

- Normalization is the process of breaking the database into smaller, more manageable tables, each table representing a single entity or concept.
- Typically, when all your tables are in BCNF, you can consider your database fully normalized. A table in BCNF must have the following features:
  - It has a primary key.
  - It has no multivalued columns.
  - All columns are dependent on a key but nothing else.
  - It contains no transitive dependency. (All its nonkey columns are directly dependent on a key.)

  In a sense, normalization involves checking your tables against the guidelines of BCNF, identifying violations, and revising your database design.
- `NOT NULL` and primary key/foreign key constraints play critical roles in your database design.
- If you may need to restructure your database design or migrate your database, name all constraints that can be named.
- To avoid using `NULL` values in a column, use the `NOT NULL` constraint.

- The UNIQUE constraint is handy if you have some nonkey columns that should all contain unique values.
- The DEFAULT constraint is handy for dealing with timestamps and placeholder values.
- The CHECK constraint can validate data format, ranges, and other complex business logic when other constraints fail.

Security | 7
and optimization

In this chapter

- You evaluate and strengthen the security of your database.

- You further improve the storage efficiency of your database design beyond normalization.

- You learn about indexing and how to apply it when implementing your database design to improve query performance.

- You learn about denormalization and apply it to your database design to further improve query performance.

What you need to know

You can find the database design covered in this chapter (it's finally complete) represented using tools commonly used by practitioners, such as dbdiagram.io and MySQL Workbench. in the GitHub repository (https://github.com/Neo-Hao/grokking-relational-database-design). You can navigate to the `chapter_07` folder and follow the instructions in the `README.md` file to load the database design into corresponding tools.

(continued)

You can also find the SQL scripts corresponding to the finalized database design for different relational database management systems (RDBMSs), including MySQL, MariaDB, PostgreSQL, SQLite, SQL Server, and Oracle.

Overview

In this chapter, you will explore database security and optimization. You will see how to evaluate the integrity and confidentiality of your database design, enhance storage efficiency beyond normalization, understand when to use denormalization, and apply indexing to improve query performance.

Security

Security is an important aspect of database design. To help safeguard the data against leaks, you need to evaluate the security of your database design and ensure that it follows at least a few key security principles. In this section, you will learn about two of those principles—integrity and confidentiality—and see how to apply them to your database design.

Integrity

Integrity involves maintaining the accuracy, completeness, and trustworthiness of data and systems. In database design, using the integrity lens to review your database design typically involves checking whether all columns, tables, and relationships are designed and implemented properly to preserve data integrity. By "designed and implemented properly," we mean that they follow the established principles of database design and implementation covered in chapters 4 to 6, such as the following:

- Every column has the best data type.
- Every table has a primary key.
- A foreign key maintains the relationship between tables.
- Constraints are based on requirement analysis.

Database design typically involves multiple iterations. It is easy to make some small mistakes or neglect something. The foreign key constraint may easily slip your mind, for example.

Imagine a database dedicated to storing authors and their books for a publishing company's web application. This database has two related tables, author and book, with the following design:

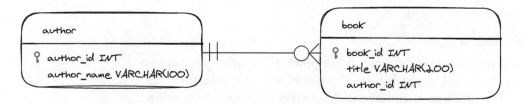

Because entity-relationship (E-R) diagrams don't represent foreign keys or other constraints, it is easy to neglect them and map the two tables to the following SQL command:

```
CREATE TABLE author (
    author_id INT PRIMARY KEY,
    author_name VARCHAR(100) NOT NULL
);
-- comment: the book table misses the
-- comment: foreign key constraints
CREATE TABLE book (
    book_id INT PRIMARY KEY,
    title VARCHAR(200) NOT NULL,
    author_id INT NOT NULL
);
```

Without a foreign key constraint, nothing prevents an orphan record in the child table from referring to a nonexistent record in the parent table. Such problems can make the database more complex to manage and secure, in turn creating gaps that attackers can exploit. To fix the preceding SQL command, you need to add the foreign key constraint to the `book` table:

```
CREATE TABLE book (
  book_id INT PRIMARY KEY,
  title VARCHAR(200) NOT NULL,
  author_id INT NOT NULL,
  CONSTRAINT FK_author_id
    FOREIGN KEY (author_id)
    REFERENCES author(author_id)
);
```

Confidentiality

Confidentiality involves protecting information from unauthorized access and disclosure, ensuring that data is accessed only by authorized people and processes. You can take two approaches to confidentiality: *access control* and *encryption*.

Access control

Using access control in databases is like posting a security guard at a club entrance. This guard decides who gets in and what areas they can access. In a database, access control determines who can view, modify, or delete data. It's essential to ensure that authorized users are given the right amount of authority to access and modify the data they should be able to control.

The two main types of access control are *mandatory access control* (MAC) and *role-based access control* (RBAC). MAC is like a strict school with rigid rules. In this system, a central authority controls who can access what data, and the rules are very tight. Every piece of data, such as a table or row, has a classification level (such as sensitive or confidential), and users are given access permissions for different classification levels. If your permission doesn't match the data's classification, you can't access it. There are no exceptions.

Think about a high school database that manages student records. In this database, tables are labeled by level of sensitivity:

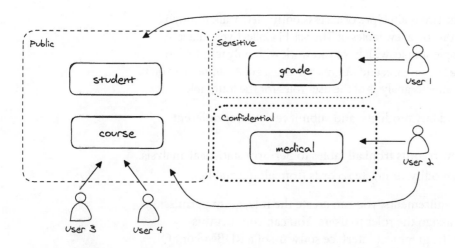

Only users with the right clearance can access tables labeled as sensitive or confidential. In MAC, sensitivity classification needs to be configured manually.

RBAC is more flexible and user-friendly. Instead of assigning permissions to users individually, RBAC assigns permissions to roles, and users are assigned to these roles. The system is like different types of membership in a club: some members can access the VIP lounge, some can access only the bar, and others can only access the general area. If RBAC is used in the high school's database, it adds an extra layer of roles:

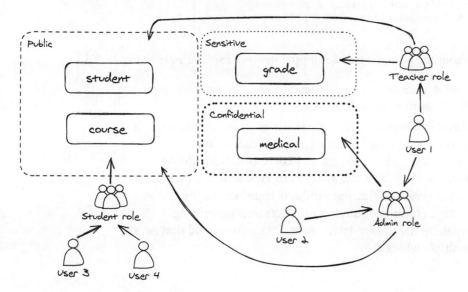

Now you know the two main types of access control, let's walk through implementing RBAC on a few tables of The Sci-Fi Collective's database. To keep this example simple, we'll have you work with only four tables: `product`, `purchase`, `review`, and `purchase_review`. Assume that you've done some requirements analysis of the user roles for the four tables:

- `USER`—View and buy products, and submit reviews for different products.
- `ANALYST`—View records from all tables to perform statistical analysis.
- `ADMIN`—View, modify, or delete records from all four tables.

Based on these requirements, you can create the role, grant permissions to the roles, and assign the roles to users. You can conduct this process by using the graphical interface software of a RDBMS or SQL commands. You can start by tackling the `USER` role:

```
-- comment: works for MySQL and MariaDB
-- comment: consult ChatGPT on adaptations
-- comment: for other RDBMS
-- step 1: create a role
CREATE ROLE standard_user;
-- step 2: grant permissions to a role
GRANT SELECT ON database_name.product TO standard_user;
GRANT INSERT ON database_name.purchase TO standard_user;
GRANT INSERT ON database_name.purchase_product
    TO standard_user;
GRANT INSERT ON database_name.review TO standard_user;
-- step 3: assign the role to a new user
CREATE USER 'morpheus'@'%' IDENTIFIED BY 'password';
GRANT standard_user TO 'morpheus'@'%';
```

A few things about the preceding code snippet deserve explanation:

- The role's name is `standard_user` instead of `user` because `user` is a reserved SQL keyword in most RDBMSs.
- A `SELECT` clause (such as `SELECT ON database_name.product`) corresponds to viewing a table, and an `INSERT` clause (such as `INSERT ON database_name.purchase`) corresponds to adding data to a table. The `USER` role allows users to view and buy products as well as submit reviews. Viewing products translates to the `GRANT SELECT ON … TO …` command; buying products and submitting reviews translate to the `GRANT INSERT ON … TO …` command that is applied to multiple tables.

- Whenever you create a new user d via the CREATE command, the standard_user role is immediately granted to that user.
- In MySQL and MariaDB, user accounts always require a host specification in the format 'username'@'host'. The 'host' portion determines where the user can connect from. 'username'@'%' allows connections from any host.

The ANALYST role can be put together as follows:

```
-- comment: works for MySQL and MariaDB
-- comment: consult ChatGPT on adaptations
-- comment: for other RDBMS
-- step 1: create a role
CREATE ROLE analyst;
-- step 2: grant permissions to a role
GRANT SELECT ON database_name.product TO analyst;
GRANT SELECT ON database_name.purchase TO analyst;
GRANT SELECT ON database_name.purchase_product
    TO analyst;
GRANT SELECT ON database_name.review TO analyst;
-- step 3: assign the role to a new user
CREATE USER 'smith'@'%' IDENTIFIED BY 'password';
GRANT analyst TO 'smith'@'%';
-- step 4: enable role by default (MySQL 8.0+)
ALTER USER 'smith'@'%' DEFAULT ROLE analyst;
```

Because the ANALYST role requires only view access to four tables, only the GRANT SELECT clause is needed here.

The ADMIN role is addressed as follows:

```
-- comment: works for MySQL and MariaDB
-- comment: consult ChatGPT on adaptations
-- comment: for other RDBMS
-- step 1: create a role
CREATE ROLE admin;
-- step 2: grant permissions to a role
GRANT SELECT, INSERT, UPDATE, DELETE
  ON database_name.product TO admin;
GRANT SELECT, INSERT, UPDATE, DELETE
  ON database_name.purchase TO admin;
GRANT SELECT, INSERT, UPDATE, DELETE
  ON database_name.purchase_product TO admin;
GRANT SELECT, INSERT, UPDATE, DELETE
  ON database_name.review TO admin;
-- step 3: assign the role to a new user
CREATE USER 'david'@'%' IDENTIFIED BY 'password';
GRANT admin TO 'david'@'%';
-- step 4: enable role by default (MySQL 8.0+)
ALTER USER 'david'@'%' DEFAULT ROLE admin;
```

Access control is an important task frequently performed by both database designers and administrators to various degrees throughout the software development process. This topic is worthy of its own chapter or a whole book that goes beyond the focus of this book (database design).

Encryption

Two types of encryption are commonly used in databases: one-way and symmetric.

One-way encryption turns data into a fixed-size, seemingly random string. This process, typically known as *hashing*, refers to a function that takes an input and returns a fixed-size string of bytes. One-way encryption is practically impossible to reverse, especially for longer values. In other words, given a hashed value derived from one-way encryption, you can't obtain its original input data.

One-way encryption is frequently used to hash passwords in databases because people typically reuse passwords everywhere. If an unauthorized person gains access to the database, they won't know what the original passwords were, so the damage won't be greatly amplified. Common one-way encryption algorithms include bcrypt, PBKDF2, and Sha512.

Your own database design includes columns that can benefit from one-way encryption. The user table has a column (password) that's dedicated to storing users' passwords. Up to now, this column has been designed to store users' passwords in plain text:

```
user

 ⚲ email VARCHAR(320)
   username VARCHAR(30)
   password VARCHAR(20)
   first_name VARCHAR(50)
   last_name VARCHAR(50)
   phone_number VARCHAR(15)
   last_login_time TIMESTAMP
```

When you apply a one-way encryption algorithm to hash all the passwords, however, you need to revise the database design accordingly. You could use the bcrypt algorithm to hash all the passwords, for example. This algorithm results in sequences of 40-byte binary data. Considering that some binary data can't be printed easily, it is common practice to further encode the binary data into a string of ASCII characters via some encoding mechanism (such as Base64) so you can store hashed passwords with the CHAR data type.

The encoded string from the 40-byte binary data will be 60 bytes long. That said, VARCHAR(20) is too small for the hashed passwords, so you have to update the data type of your password column to CHAR(60):

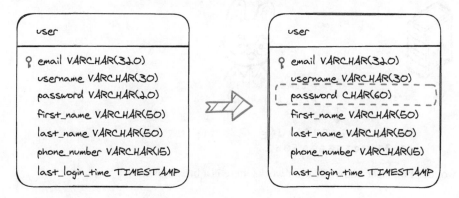

If you have already implemented your database design, you can use the following SQL command to update your user table:

```
-- comment: works for MySQL and MariaDB
-- comment: consult ChatGPT on adaptations
-- comment: for other RDBMS
ALTER TABLE user MODIFY COLUMN password CHAR(60);
```

Unhashing the mystery

A *hash function* is a mathematical function that takes a variable-length input (such as a password) and produces a fixed-length output: the hash. The function is one-way, so you won't see the word *unhashing* in any dictionary! Hash functions have many uses, but the hash functions we cover here are used specifically for encryption.

(*continued*)

Plain passwords in databases that are compromised can be stolen and reused elsewhere, which is why good database design dictates that passwords be stored in hash form. Many hash functions are well known and standardized (such as Sha512 and bcrypt). Even hashed passwords can be vulnerable, though, because an attacker may try a brute-force attack (try random passwords through the hash function) or use a rainbow table (a list of known passwords and their precalculated hashes). ost applications would concatenate a password with a *salt* (random string) that is stored or produced by the application. An attacker has no means of deducing what the password is without knowing the salt.

In case if you wonder how user authentication works, here is a breakdown of the process:

1. The application takes the password that the user provides during the login process and hashes it in the same approach.

2. The application compares the hashed result with what is already stored in the database. If the hashed result matches the hash stored in the database, the user is authenticated.

In contrast to one-way encryption, *symmetric encryption* is reversible. In other words, when a symmetric encryption algorithm is used for encryption, the encrypted value can be decrypted to retrieve the original input data.

Symmetric encryption is commonly used to protect sensitive information that needs to be used repeatedly and/or periodically in its original form. Online stores, for example, want to protect users' data, so they don't users' credit card information in plain text. Online stores also want to make users' lives easier by allowing them to save and reuse credit cards for the next order. As a result, symmetric encryption is used to encrypt credit card information to keep it safe in the database. When a user wants to reuse a credit card for a transaction, the application can always decrypt the stored value. Symmetric encryption achieves encryption and decryption by using the same key and same algorithm in the process of encryption and decryption. The key is typically a string of characters or numbers, and the security of symmetric encryption relies on the secrecy and proper handling of this key.

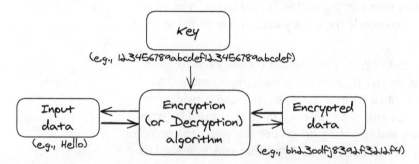

Common symmetric algorithms include Advanced Encryption Standard (AES), Triple DES (3DES), and Blowfish. Each algorithm has a set of variants. Depending on the key length (such as 128 bits, 192 bits, or 256 bits), AES has three variants: AES-128, AES-192, and AES-256. The key length determines the level of security and the computational requirements for encryption and decryption. The longer the key is, the higher the security and computational requirements are.

Can any columns in your own database design can benefit from symmetric encryption? Yes. The `payment_method` table stores some columns of sensitive information that can be reused repeatedly, such as `card_number` and `expiry_date`. The two columns represent the credit card information required to place an order. Up to now, they've been set to store everything in plain text:

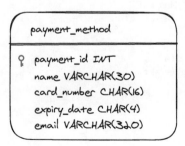

If you want to store encrypted data instead of plain text, you must revise the database design. You could use AES-256 to encrypt `card_number` first. AES-256 operates on blocks of 16 bytes. The `card_number` is 16 bytes, which is one block in ES-256. AES algorithms commonly use *initialization vectors* (IVs) to further enhance security. You can think of an IV as a nonsecret 16-byte binary sequence used as an additional input. When IV is used, the input data is 32-byte. As in one-way encryption, the encrypted data is binary, and it is common to further encode the binary data into a string of ASCII characters. Assuming that Base64 was used to encode the binary data, the encoded string is about 45-byte.

What about `expiry_date`? AES-256 operates on blocks of 16 bytes; when the plain text is shorter than 16 bytes, padding is required to make the plain text fit into a 16-byte block, so AES-256 considers the lengths of `expiry_date` and `card_number` to be the same (16 bytes). If the same encryption and encoding procedure is applied, the encoded and encrypted string will all be about 45-byte. That said, you need to update the data types of both columns to CHAR(45):

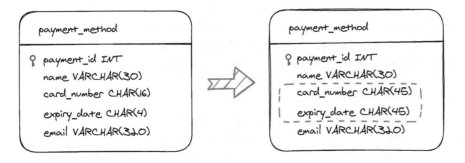

If you have already implemented your database design, you can use the following SQL command to update your `payment_method` table:

```
-- comment: works for MySQL and MariaDB
-- comment: consult ChatGPT on adaptations
-- comment: for other RDBMS
ALTER TABLE payment_method
   MODIFY COLUMN card_number CHAR(45),
   MODIFY COLUMN expiry_date CHAR(45);
```

Symmetric encryption: Not the panacea

Symmetric encryption seems to be more convenient than one-way encryption because it supports both encryption and decryption. You may wonder why we don't use symmetric encryption to encrypt passwords and all other information that requires protection. Symmetric encryption should not be used to encrypt passwords. To take this discussion one step further, if the sensitive data doesn't need to be used repeatedly in its original form, you shouldn't consider symmetric encryption.

One-way encryption is typically stronger than symmetric encryption. Symmetric encryption works on a big assumption: the key used for encryption and decryption is safe. If a hacker somehow gains access to the key, all the sensitive information encrypted with symmetric encryption could be in danger because everything can be reversed and the original data exposed.

As a result, storage of the key in symmetric encryption is critical. You don't want to store this key in the same database as the encrypted data, for example. In the real world, this key is stored in various ways, such as the following:

- Via environmental variables in a file in the application server

- Via dedicated software known as a *key management service*

- Via a specialized physical device known as a *hardware security module*

Storage considerations

After a database is designed, revised, implemented, and tested, it goes into production and starts costing money. You need to think about not only read and write operations but also efficient use of storage.

Historically, storage was expensive. In the 1970s, 1 MB of storage could cost about $250. The cost of that same megabyte today is about $0.00001.

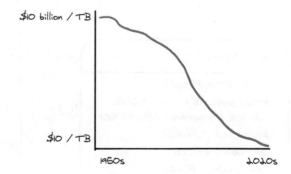

Despite this trend, improving your database design to save storage space can still be valuable, especially if you are designing the database for a scalable application that millions of people will use or that may experience exponential growth.

What do you do in database design to save storage? Reduce data redundancy. You have already done a lot in this respect. Normalization addresses anomalies as well as reduces data redundancy. Beyond normalization, you may find opportunities in your design to further reduce data redundancy in your design, as you will see in this section.

Redundant tables

Your database design for The Sci-Fi Collective is normalized. But a normalized design can still be improved to reduce redundancy.

When you review your design and check for redundancies, you can start by asking a simple question: are there any redundant (or almost redundant) tables? The answer is yes. If you focus on how addresses are stored, you see two tables that are almost identical:

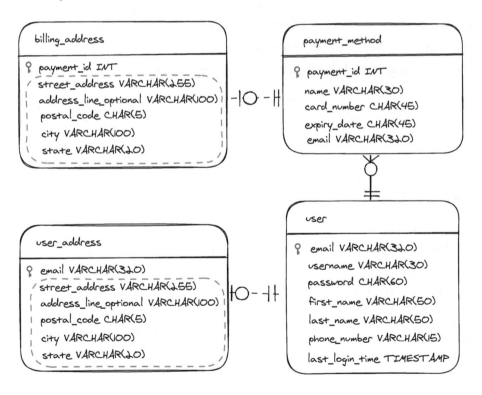

The tables `billing_address` and `user_address` have nearly identical columns except for the primary key. This design is legit because an address associated with a payment method may not be the same as a user's personal address. It is highly likely, however, that a user and their payment methods share an address, so it would be nice to consolidate that data.

How do you proceed? A good start is to analyze and update the requirements. To consolidate address data, you can use a single address entity that stores a single address that both the `user` and `payment_method` tables can point to or two different addresses so that you don't have to store the same address in two different tables. Based on this change, the requirements that need to be fulfilled need further clarification:

- A user has one address.
- A payment method has one address.
- An address is associated with zero to many users or zero to many payment methods.

It's not hard to map the requirements to an E-R diagram. If you use a single entity (such as `address`) to represent addresses, what should be its primary key? If you remember what you learned in chapter 4, you need a real-world concept to differentiate two addresses—a combination of all columns, including `street_address`, `address_line_optional`, `postal_code`, `city`, and `state`. Using a composite primary key composed of all columns is generally considered bad design for two reasons:

- A composite key composed of every column significantly drags down performance.
- The `address` entity is in a one-to-many relationship with `user` and `payment_method`. The choice of this composite key will force you to put every column of `address` in `user` and `payment_method`.

As a result, you may choose an alternative to the composite key: surrogate key plus unique constraint. In chapter 4, you learned that a surrogate key is often implemented as an autoincrementing numeric attribute (such as `address_id`), which is simple, flexible, and easy to use as a single-column foreign key. The unique constraint will be placed on the combination of all columns except the surrogate key (`address_id`) to ensure that no redundant address data can be recorded in the `address` table.

Now that you have nailed nearly every bit of the revised design, you are ready to map the revised requirements to an E-R diagram:

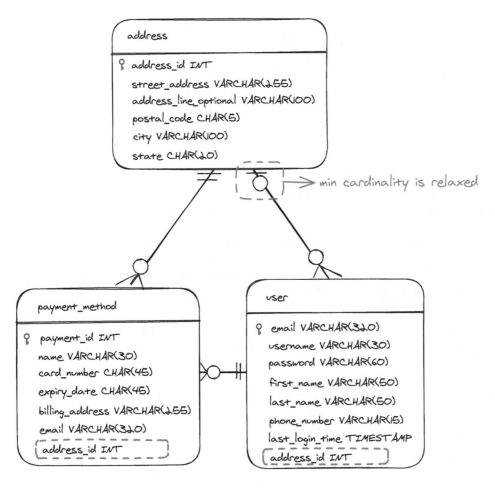

It is worth noting that the min cardinality of the relationship from `user` to `address` tables is relaxed from one to zero. This relaxation is a must, considering that users will register accounts with The Sci-Fi Collective without providing personal address information. If the min cardinality of this relationship stays as one, it will prevent user data from being recorded in the `user` table without a corresponding `address` row.

If you have already implemented your database design, you need to take three steps to update your implementation:

1. Drop two old tables, `billing_address` and `user_address`.
2. Create a new table named `address`, and add a unique constraint to the combination of all nonkey columns.
3. Update `payment_method` and `user` by adding a new column. `address_id`, and making it a foreign key in both tables.

To create the `address` table, you can use the following command:

```
-- comment: works for MySQL and MariaDB
-- comment: see the code repo for other RDBMS
CREATE TABLE IF NOT EXISTS address (
  address_id INT AUTO_INCREMENT PRIMARY KEY,
  street_address VARCHAR(255) NOT NULL,
  address_line_optional VARCHAR(100),
  city VARCHAR(100) NOT NULL,
  state VARCHAR(20) NOT NULL,
  postal_code CHAR(5) NOT NULL,
  CONSTRAINT unique_address_constraint
    UNIQUE (street_address, address_line_optional,
            postal_code, city, state)
);
```

To update the `payment_method` table, you can use the following command:

```
-- comment: works for MySQL, MariaDB, and PostgreSQL
-- comment: consult ChatGPT on adaptations
-- comment: for other RDBMS
ALTER TABLE payment_method
  ADD COLUMN address_id INT NOT NULL;

ALTER TABLE payment_method
  ADD CONSTRAINT fk_address_payment_method
    FOREIGN KEY (address_id)
    REFERENCES address(address_id);
```

By contrast, the `address_id` won't have the NOT NULL constraint in the `user` table because of the relaxed min cardinality of the relationship from `user` to `address`. Moreover, you need to ensure that the `address_id` column starts with a NULL value by default:

```
-- comment: works for MySQL, MariaDB, and PostgreSQL
-- comment: consult ChatGPT on adaptations
-- comment: for other RDBMS
ALTER TABLE user
  ADD COLUMN address_id INT NULL;
```

```
ALTER TABLE user
  ADD CONSTRAINT fk_address_user
    FOREIGN KEY (address_id)
    REFERENCES address(address_id);
```

NULL values in foreign key columns represent optional relationships, which is the business logic you want. In other words, not every record in the child table (user) needs to have a corresponding link in the referenced parent table (address). That logic also means, however, that you need to be extra-cautious in handling NULL values when querying the two tables.

Categorical data

After checking and dealing with redundant tables, you can go one step further by checking for columns that contain redundant data. When you review your database design, you can try a different question: Is there a column that contains a lot of redundant data? Yes.

If you focus on the address table that you just added, you see that the state column contains a lot of redundant data. After all, The Sci-Fi Collective has millions of users, and there are only 50 states plus Washington, DC, in the United States. (In chapter 4, we assumed that The Sci-Fi Collective sells only in the United States.)

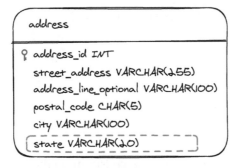

How do you address this problem? You can move the state column from the address table to a new table named state and link the two tables via a relationship. This new table, named state, will represent all 50 states plus the District of Columbia, and it will be in a one-to-many relationship with the address table.

What would be the primary key for the state table? Every state plus the District of Columbia has its own abbreviation, and the abbreviations are different but have the same length. As a result, the abbreviation is the perfect primary key for the `state` table:

Alabama: AL
Alaska: AK
...
California: CA
Colorado: CO
...
District of Columbia: DC

Based on the preceding revision, your updated `address` table and new `state` table will look like this:

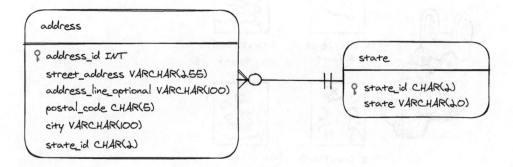

As you learned in chapter 5, you need to relax the min cardinality of the relationship from `state` to `address` a little to enable data entry.

Indexing

Now that you have taken action to further reduce data redundancy in your database design, it is time to work on making data retrieval efficient. *Indexing* is a critical optimization technique used to speed retrieval of data from a database. When implementing a database design, you need to index certain columns to speed tasks such as data retrieval, sorting, and searching. In this section, you will learn why and how to index; then you will decide whether you need to index certain columns in your own database design.

Why and how to index

Several types of indexing are used to optimize query performance in databases, such as standard indexes, clustered indexes, spatial indexes, and full-text indexes. In this section, you will learn why and how to implement standard and full-text indexes.

Standard indexes

To index properly, you need to understand why indexes are important and what problems they address. Let's start with a simple `movie` table in a database that supports a movie application:

The silence of the Yams

Beauty and the Feast

The Shawshank Rejection

Gone with the Gin

The design of the `movie` table looks like this:

Notice that the application frequently sorts all movies by ratings because users always want to watch the highest-rated movies. As a result, your application frequently takes advantage of the following query:

```
-- comment: works for MySQL, MariaDB,
-- comment: PostgreSQL and SQLite
-- comment: consult ChatGPT on adaptations
-- comment: for other RDBMS
SELECT *
  FROM movie
  ORDER BY rating DESC
  LIMIT 30;
```

The query is executed clause by clause in the following order:

1. FROM—The query begins with the FROM clause. The database system identifies the movie table from which the data will be retrieved and reads data from the table.
2. SELECT—The SELECT clause selects every column for each row.
3. ORDER BY—ORDER BY sorts all the rows in the movie table by rating in descending order.
4. LIMIT—Finally, the LIMIT 30 clause restricts the output to the first 30 rows of the ordered list.

Without the help of indexes, this query needs to sort all movies by rating from scratch every time this query is executed. If the movie table holds millions of records and keeps growing, you can imagine how easy it is for this query to affect the performance of the database and slow the application. To address this problem, you can index the rating column:

```
CREATE INDEX idx_rating ON movie (rating);
```

What does an index do? An index creates additional data structures that provide fast access to rows based on the values in one or more columns. Indexes are typically implemented with data structures such as B-trees. A *B-tree* is a self-balancing tree data structure that maintains sorted data and allows searches, sequential access, insertions, and deletions in logarithmic time. When an index is created on a column, the database engine constructs the index by scanning the entire table and recording the values of the indexed column along with pointers to the corresponding rows. In our case, when the index on the rating column is constructed, it will be used to speed queries that sort or search for a value in the rating column of the movie table:

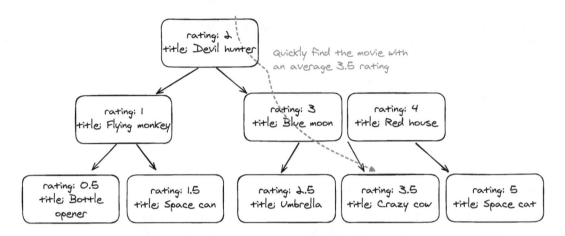

It is worth mentioning that all queries that use the WHERE clause to filter data based on ratings perform searching tasks and are be optimized by the index you added on the rating column:

```
SELECT *
  FROM movie
  WHERE rating = 5;
```

Similarly, if you foresee or observe that users often sort or search for movies by release date, and the application frequently executes the query

```
-- comment: works for MySQL, MariaDB,
-- comment: PostgreSQL and SQLite
-- comment: consult ChatGPT on adaptations
-- comment: for other RDBMS
SELECT *
  FROM movie
  ORDER BY date DESC
  LIMIT 30;
```

you may want to index the date column too:

```
CREATE INDEX idx_rating ON movie (date);
```

If the application allows users to sort movies by both release date and rating, and the application frequently executes the query

```
-- comment: works for MySQL, MariaDB,
-- comment: PostgreSQL and SQLite
-- comment: consult ChatGPT on adaptations
-- comment: for other RDBMS
SELECT *
  FROM movie
```

```
ORDER BY date DESC, rating DESC
LIMIT 30;
```

you may want to index the combination of the `rating` and `date` columns too:

```
CREATE INDEX idx_combo ON movie (rating, date);
```

In all those cases, the columns that were explicitly indexed are not the primary key. What if the primary key requires indexing? Well, the primary key `movie_id` column is already indexed. All primary keys are indexed automatically.

Full-text indexes

A `CREATE INDEX` statement creates standard indexes, which are suitable for speeding many tasks, such as sorting and exact matches. Occasionally, however, you will find that standard indexes aren't sufficient for some indexing tasks. Your movie application may allow users to search for movies by titles, and the search bar needs to support keyword searching, partial word matching, and even fuzzy searching (handling typos or misspellings).

When you need to support complex search on text, you need *full-text indexes*, which make all such tasks much more efficient. In short, full-text indexes tokenize each word or term and then store each token in a lookup table. Without full-text indexing, keyword searching would look like this example:

```
SELECT *
  FROM movie
  WHERE title LIKE '%exciting%';
```

As you can imagine, even if this search is doable, it is inefficient. As the data size grows, this query takes longer to execute. With full-text indexing, the same task is much faster and looks like this:

```
-- comment: works for MySQL and MariaDB
-- comment: consult ChatGPT on adaptations
-- comment: for other RDBMS
-- comment: add a full-text index
CREATE FULLTEXT INDEX ft_idx_title
  ON movie (title);
-- comment: search
SELECT *
  FROM movie
  WHERE MATCH(title)
  AGAINST('exciting' IN NATURAL LANGUAGE MODE);
```

Although the concept of a full-text index is consistent across RDBMSs, the syntax varies significantly from one RDBMS to another. The preceding SQL command adds a full-text index for the `title` column in the `movie` table and works for MySQL and MariaDB. By contrast, to achieve the same thing in PostgreSQL, you need to use the following code:

```
-- comment: works for PostgreSQL
-- comment: consult ChatGPT on adaptations
-- comment: for other RDBMS
-- comment: add a full-text index
ALTER TABLE movie ADD COLUMN tsv_title;
UPDATE movie
  SET tsv_title = to_tsvector('english', title);
CREATE INDEX gin_idx_title
  ON movie USING gin(tsv_title);
```

If you want to figure out how to add a full-text index in a specific RDBMS, ChatGPT is a great friend.

Indexes for your ER diagram

To explore whether you can use indexes to optimize your database design, you need to understand what queries are generated by the application logic. This step may require close collaboration between you (the database designer) and application developers, especially backend engineers. In this process, backend engineers can do the following things:

- Contribute detailed knowledge of how the application interacts with the database, especially queries generated by the application logic.
- Provide insights into performance bottlenecks observed during application runtime and user interactions.
- Ensure that changes in application logic or new features align with best practices of database design.

During the collaboration, you will do the following things:

- Understand how to structure the database and design indexes to optimize these queries, and use the shared information to adjust database design, create appropriate indexes, and optimize query execution plans.
- Ensure that database schema changes do not negatively affect application performance or lead to inconsistencies.

- Ensure that database-schema changes meet the customer's requirements (unless the requirements have changed).

Beyond collaborating with application developers, database designers commonly take empirical approaches to identify indexing opportunities by synthesizing data from query performance metrics and query logs when the implemented database goes into production. If you have identified opportunities to use indexes, the following three examples show what you need to do next.

The product table

For the product table, you've identified one interaction scenario:

Users search for products based on their name.

```
product

🔑  code CHAR(12)
    name VARCHAR(100)
    description TEXT
    manufacturer VARCHAR(100)
    photo VARCHAR(1000)
    price DECIMAL(7, 2)
    cost DECIMAL(7, 2)
    inventory_quantity INT
```

This scenario corresponds to the following query:

```
-- comment: works with MySQL and MariaDB
-- comment: consult ChatGPT on adaptations
-- comment: for other RDBMS
SELECT * FROM product WHERE MATCH (name)
  AGAINST ('some text' IN NATURAL LANGUAGE MODE);
```

This query performs a keyword search task on the name column. To make the query possible and efficient, add a full-text index to this column:

```
-- comment: works for MySQL and MariaDB
-- comment: consult ChatGPT on adaptations
-- comment: for other RDBMS
CREATE FULLTEXT INDEX ft_idx_name ON product (name);
```

The review table

For the `review` table, you've identified the following interaction between users and the application:

> Users frequently check product reviews.

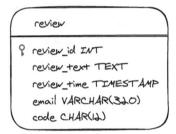

This interaction leads to frequent queries of the `review` table. When a user tries to check the reviews of a product with code `23356`, for example, the following query is executed:

```
SELECT * FROM review WHERE code = '23356';
```

This query is a search task, but only because an exact match is involved. In other words, if this column ever needs indexing, standard indexing would be good enough. Indexing would improve the efficiency of this query. The `code` column in the `review` table is a foreign key, and foreign key columns are not indexed automatically. As a result, you can index this column as follows:

```
CREATE INDEX idx_code ON review (code);
```

The payment_method table

For the `payment_method` table, you've identified the following scenario:

> Users always need to select one of their many added payment methods frequently to complete a transaction.

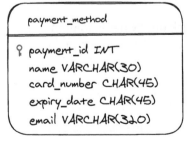

This interaction leads to frequent queries of the `payment_method` table. When a user with the email address john@gmail.com tries to access his payment methods, for example, the following query executes:

```
SELECT * FROM payment_method
   WHERE email = 'john@gmail.com';
```

This query is also a search task that involves an exact match. The `email` column in the `payment_method` table is a foreign key. Standard indexing on this column would be good enough:

```
CREATE INDEX idx_email ON payment_method (email);
```

Denormalization

So far, you have put a lot of effort into optimizing a database. Now we are going to talk about edge cases in which optimization means actively going against normalization. Yes, you read that right!

How to denormalize

Denormalization is a last-ditch database optimization technique that intentionally introduces redundancy to a database to improve query performance. Denormalization is rare, but if queries are performed frequently and require joining multiple tables, denormalization can significantly enhance the performance of your database.

Denormalization typically involves two steps:

1. Identify queries that are used frequently and require joining more than two tables.
2. Duplicating some columns in some tables involved in the identified query to reduce the number of tables that have to be joined.

To get a better understanding of denormalization, consider an oversimplified example first. Suppose that you oversee a database supporting a music app, and you have three tables representing artists, albums, and songs in your database:

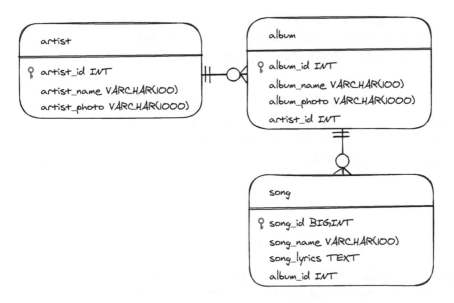

From the relationships among the tables, you can tell that songs are organized by albums and albums are organized by artists. You can also tell that the three tables are fully normalized. But the application supported by the database often needs to display the top songs for every artist:

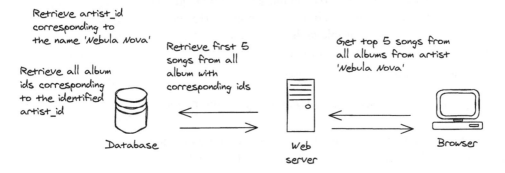

Because of the relationships among the three tables, you need to join them to map songs to artists. As a result, the following query has to be executed frequently:

```
-- comment: works for MySQL, MariaDB,
-- comment: and PostgreSQL
-- comment: consult ChatGPT on adaptations
```

```
-- comment: for other RDBMS
SELECT artist.artist_name, song.song_title
  FROM artist
  INNER JOIN album
    ON artist.artist_id = album.artist_id
  INNER JOIN song
    ON album.album_id = song.album_id
  WHERE artist.artist_name = 'Nebula Nova'
  ORDER BY album.album_id, song.song_id
  LIMIT 5;
```

Because of the sizes of the three tables and the high frequency of the query, this query may take more time and resources to run than you expect. As a result, the pages or screens that require help from this query become less responsive in your application. Further, this query costs a lot of resources and money whenever it runs.

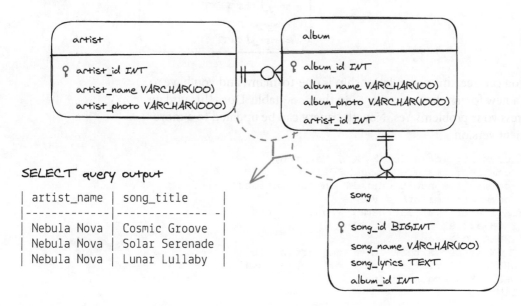

How do you address this problem? You may notice that the `album` table doesn't contribute any data to the output data. Due to how the three tables are related, you still need to join all three tables to get what you want. If a direct relationship exists between `artist` and `song`, this query will become much more efficient. Create this relationship, and update the E-R diagram of the three tables:

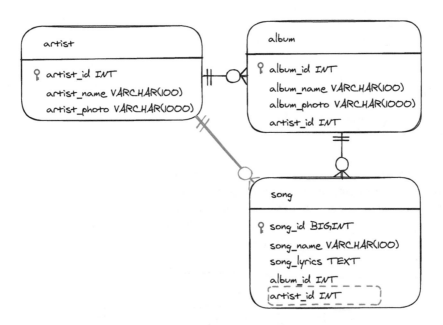

As you can see, this new relationship is one-to-many, and you have to add a new foreign key, `artist_i`, to the `song` table. Does this update address your problem? Yes. Now the query can be updated to a more efficient version:

```
-- comment: works for MySQL, MariaDB,
-- comment: PostgreSQL and SQLite
-- comment: consult ChatGPT on adaptations
-- comment: for other RDBMS
SELECT artist.artist_name, song.song_title
  FROM artist
  INNER JOIN song
    ON artist.artist_id = song.artist_id
  WHERE artist.artist_name = 'Nebula Nova'
  ORDER BY song.song_id
  LIMIT 5;
```

This update, however, introduces a new problem: it creates a transitive dependency in the `song` table:

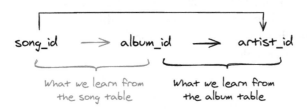

You deliberately introduced redundancy to the `song` table to make a normalized design abnormal—hence, the name *denormalization*. Sometimes, you have to weigh the benefits and costs of sticking to a fully normalized design and tolerating some abnormal tables when you need to improve query efficiency and database performance.

It's important to know that denormalization has the potential to compromise data integrity if it is not managed meticulously. When redundant data exists across denormalized tables, any alterations of the data may require updates of all related tables.

After denormalization, you still need to pay close attention to database performance to validate your move. If a significant volume of `INSERT`, `UPDATE`, and `DELETE` operations occur on related tables, the performance benefits of denormalization may diminish quickly, and you may need to reevaluate the situation.

Comprehensive documentation and effective communication are crucial to denormalizing a database design. After all, denormalization can be a debatable, controversial move. To get other people to buy into this change, you have to communicate the denormalization strategy to members of the development team, stakeholders, and other interested parties to establish shared understanding and ensure consistent implementation. More important, to prevent future problems or accidents, you want to thoroughly document the denormalization strategy, outlining the rationale, tradeoffs, and factors that influenced the denormalization decisions.

Denormalize your database design

Take a look at your database design to see whether denormalization can be useful anywhere. Specifically, you want to look at the `user`, `payment_method,` and `purchase` tables, as shown in the following figure.

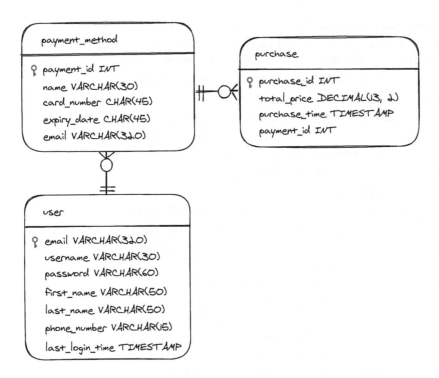

In an online store like The Sci-Fi Collective's, users commonly check their orders or receipts. Whenever that happens, the application queries the preceding three tables:

```
SELECT * FROM purchase
  INNER JOIN payment_method
    ON purchase.payment_method_id =
      payment_method.payment_method_id
  INNER JOIN user
    ON purchase.user_id = user.user_id
  WHERE user.email = 'customerCat@humor.com';
```

Apparently, the `payment_method` table barely contributes to the output data but has to be joined with the other two tables so that a purchase can be mapped to a corresponding user. If you recall from chapter 6, we removed the direct relationship between `user` and `purchase` when we focused on normalizing the database design. If you have abundant evidence showing that the preceding query is executed frequently, costing significant money and resources and slowing the application, you need to think again about whether to restore the direct relationship between `user` and `purchase` (in other words, to denormalize your database design):

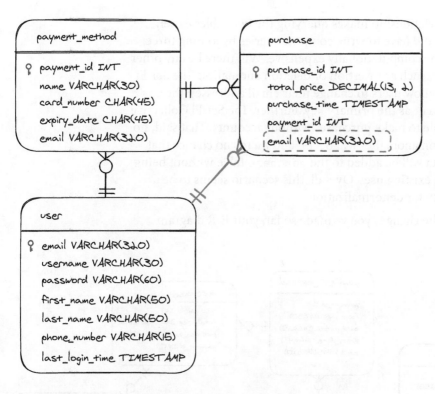

Undoubtedly, this change will introduce redundancy and create a violation of Boyce-Codd Normal Form (BCNF; see chapter 6) in the `purchase` table:

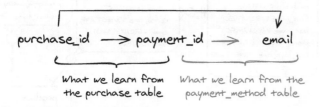

If you focus on the `purchase` table, you see a transitive dependency in which `purchase_id` determines `payment_id` and `payment_id` determines `email`.

Typically, you have to conduct a thorough cost-and-benefit analysis to evaluate whether the improved database performance is worth the trouble. A busy online store needs to generate receipts that frequently associate purchase data with a user, of course, and the direct `user-purchase` relationship makes querying the two tables easier. Without it, you would have to write complex queries by joining three tables, which can be computationally expensive. Will there be any other difficult challenges, such as insertion or deletion anomalies? The Sci-Fi Collective doesn't allow users to change their email addresses; the `user` table even uses `email` as the primary key. Further, The Sci-Fi Collective doesn't allow people to make purchases without accounts. That said, no insertion or deletion anomalies will occur, and there's no chance that some purchase data will be added to the `purchase` table without being associated with an existing user. Overall, this scenario seems to be a perfect opportunity for denormalization.

Summarizing all the changes you've made so far, your E-R diagram looks like this:

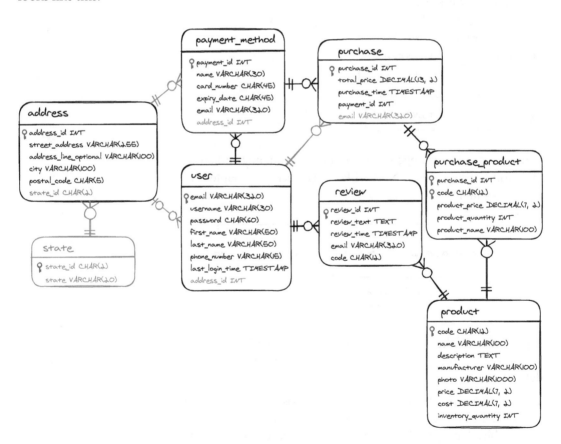

If you have made it to this point in your journey through database design, you've done an amazing job! Each chapter in this book has built on the previous one, guiding you through the intricate processes that transform disconnected ideas and requirements into structured, efficient, powerful databases. Your perseverance in understanding and applying these principles of database design is a testament to your commitment and is truly commendable. Well done!

Recap

- You shouldn't save sensitive information in plain text. Instead, pick the right encryption method, encrypt the data, and ensure that the corresponding columns have enough room for the encrypted data in your database design.
- Beyond normalization, you may have opportunities to further improve the storage efficiency of your database design. These opportunities may involve redundant tables, columns, or categorical data. Be careful, though, because you don't want to negatively affect your database performance.
- Indexing can contribute to increasing the query performance of your database. You need to work closely with the application developers and use log data to understand where to apply indexes. If you aim to support queries that involve only sorting and exact-match searching, standard indexing is good enough. But if you aim to support queries that involve keyword searching, partial word matching, or fuzzy searching, you need full-text searching.
- Denormalization deliberately introduces redundancy to improve query efficiency. Denormalization is rare and requires you to be careful about handling data insertion, updates, and deletions in the same table.

Part 3
Database design and AI

Welcome to the future of database design! In this part, you'll discover how to enhance your database design process with the power of generative AI. You'll learn how to collaborate effectively with AI tools to accelerate your design workflow while maintaining control of the process.

Chapter 8 guides you through the complexities of database design in the age of generative AI. You'll explore practical ways to integrate AI into your design process, ensuring efficiency without sacrificing quality or control.

Prepare to sharpen your skills and broaden your knowledge as you create a fully functional database from the ground up.

Database design
in the age of generative AI | **8**

In this chapter

- You explore how to use generative AI to speed database design.

- You learn how to fine-tune the prompts to get precisely what you want from generative AI tools.

- You go through the full pipeline to design and implement a database for a spaceship manufacturer with the help of generative AI tools.

What you need to know

This chapter is different from others in a major way. You are unlikely to replicate the demonstrated interactions with large language models (LLMs) due to their probabilistic nature and continuous changes. When we wrote this chapter, we used ChatGPT 4o. That said, ChatGPT may get your design exactly right or wrong in different ways even if you use the prompts demonstrated in this chapter.

(*continued*)

The database design covered in this chapter (it's finally complete), using tools commonly used by practitioners, such as dbdiagram.io and MySQL Workbench, can be found in the GitHub repository (https://github.com/Neo-Hao/grokking-relational-database-design). Navigate to the `chapter_08` folder and follow the instructions in the `README.md` file to load the database design into corresponding tools.

Also, you can find the full-text prompts for ChatGPT and SQL scripts corresponding to the final database design for different relational database management systems (RDBMS), including MySQL, MariaDB, PostgreSQL, SQLite, SQL Server, and Oracle.

Overview

In this chapter, you will explore how to take advantage of generative AI to speed database design, and you will see what a typical workflow looks like when you're working toward a complete database design with help from generative AI.

You picked up all the essentials for designing a robust database in the previous seven chapters by working on the database of The Sci-Fi Collective. It is time for a change. In this chapter, you will design a database for a company that manufactures spaceships. By working on this new project from scratch, you will start to appreciate how generative AI tools can make your life easier and understand their limitations in delivering what you expect.

Quite a few LLMs can serve our purposes, such as ChatGPT, Claude, Google Gemini, and Llama. We will use ChatGPT (GPT-4o) to demonstrate our interactions with a generative AI tool in this chapter. Due to the way ChatGPT models were trained, specific prompt formats and practices work particularly well and lead to more useful responses.

Following are three rules of thumb for working with ChatGPT:

- *Be specific, descriptive, and as detailed as possible.* All LLMs, including ChatGPT, can't be seven steps ahead of you and know what you truly want to ask when your question or request is vague or imprecise. How ChatGPT responds to your questions and instructions is captured by the age-old adage "Garbage in, garbage out." This axiom may sound familiar if you are in the field of computer science or software engineering.
- *Separate instructions from context.* Most LLMs work better when you separate instructions from context. ChatGPT hopes that you'll put instructions at the beginning of a prompt and use ### or """ to separate them from the context. When you need to summarize some long text passages in bullet points, for example, here is what ChatGPT recommends:

ChatGPT GPT-4o

Summarize the text below as a bullet-point list of the most important points.

Text: """

some long texts go here

"""

- *Articulate the desired output format through examples.* ChatGPT responds better when you give it specific format requirements. This practice also makes it easier to programmatically parse out multiple outputs reliably. When you need to summarize some long text passages in a few target entities, here is what ChatGPT recommends:

ChatGPT GPT-4o

Extract the important entities mentioned in the text below. Extract all company names, people names, and specific topics which fit the content and the general overarching themes

Desired format:

Company names: `<comma_separated_list>`

People names: – | | –

Specific topics: – | | –

General themes: – | | –

Text: " " "

some long texts go here

" " "

You can read more about recommended practices for using ChatGPT at https://mng.bz/QD41. In our experience, the three rules of thumb are most important and helpful for database design.

Before you start the database design, we want to emphasize that you shouldn't dwell on replicating the interactions with ChatGPT demonstrated in the chapter. The same request doesn't necessarily lead to the same answer for many reasons, including randomness, previous context, and model updates or refinements. Instead, focus on learning how to use ChatGPT efficiently, what working with ChatGPT looks like, and when to rely on your own judgment.

Requirements analysis

In line with the galactic theme, you will design a database for a company named SHIPS R US that specializes in manufacturing spaceships. SHIPS R US distributes spaceships in large batches to dealers across the galaxy, who eventually sell the spaceships to customers. A good analogy is how Toyota and Ford sell cars. Like those companies, SHIPS R US requires a web application powered by a database to manage all the relevant information, such as spaceship models, production records, and dealer and customer information. Your task is to design a database for this web application.

For the sake of brevity, we'll assume that you've applied all the techniques you learned in chapter 3 to collect and analyze the requirements of the SHIPS R US database. The synthesized high-level requirements are

- The database needs to maintain records on all spaceship brands and models, manufactured spaceships, dealers, customers, and relationships between dealers and customers.
- A spaceship brand is associated with multiple models, and a model is associated with multiple spacecraft.
- One or more spaceships are distributed to a dealer, who serves one or more customers.
- A customer is served by one or more dealers and is associated with one or more spaceships that they bought from the dealer(s.)
- A spaceship is associated with one model and can be associated with no more than one owner and no more than one dealer.

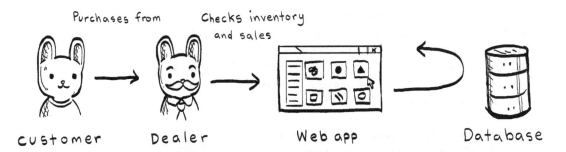

These requirements focus on entities and their relationships. Beyond this summary, you have another set of requirements focusing on entities and attributes (explored further in the next section).

Entities and attributes

In this section, you design entities and attributes based on the requirement analysis with the help of ChatGPT.

Entities

Based on the high-level requirement summary, you extracted five entities: brand, model, spaceship, dealer, and customer. If this fact is not obvious to you or you want to see how capable ChatGPT is, you can make the following request to ChatGPT:

> I am designing a database. Help me identify all the entities based on the given requirements.
>
> **Requirements: """**
>
> The database needs to maintain records of all spaceship brands and models, manufactured spaceships, dealers, customers, and relationships between dealers and customers.
>
> A spaceship brand is associated with multiple models, and a model is associated with multiple spacecrafts.
>
> A dealer is distributed one or more spaceships and serves one or more customers.
>
> A customer is served by one or more dealers and is associated with one or more spaceships that they bought from the dealers.

A spaceship is associated with one model and can be associated with no more than one owner and no more than one dealer.

" " "

As you can see from this request, we deliberately separated the instructions from the context to get better answers from ChatGPT. This question is so simple that separating instructions from context does very little, but it is a good idea to stick to the rules of thumb, and it will make a difference when you have a much more complicated question or request. Overall, the answer you get from ChatGPT will be similar to the one shown in this image:

Attributes

You worked hard on requirement analysis and have a set of synthesized requirements to help you identify the attributes of each entity:

- *A brand has a name.* The number of brands is limited and smaller than five.
- *A model has a four-digit number and name.* The number is unique per model.
- *A spaceship has a 17-digit serial number (like a vehicle identification number for a car), a recommended price, and a year number.* The serial number is unique per spaceship. The unit for the recommended price is US dollars (USD). The year number represents the year in which the spaceship was manufactured.
- *A dealer has a name, address, phone number, email address, and dealer website URL.* The dealer may be anywhere on Earth.
- *A customer has a name, address, phone number, and email address.* Multiple customers may share an address. The customer may live anywhere on Earth.

Developing the entity-relationship (E-R) diagram is a milestone in database design, requiring you to identify the attributes and their corresponding data types as well as the primary key for each entity. This step can be tedious and requires you to dig deep into the details of the gathered requirements. ChatGPT can offer help. You could use the preceding requirements for attributes to formulate the following request:

I am designing a database for a manufacturer of spaceships. I have identified five entities: brand, model, spaceship, dealer, and customer. Help me identify attributes and the primary key per entity based on the given requirements. Generate output using the desired format.

Desired format:

Entity name: spaceship

Attributes:

Serial number: CHAR(17)

Recommended price: NUMERIC(8, 2)

Primary key: Serial number

Requirements: """

A brand has a name ...... The customer may live anywhere on Earth.

  (This is an excerpt. Full text can be found at https://bit.ly/grdb.)

"""

As you can see from this request, we added the desired format for the output, which increases the consistency of the output and makes sure that it is ready to use for future interactions with ChatGPT. Following is a sample answer from ChatGPT to this request:

ChatGPT GPT-4o

Entity name: Brand

Attributes:

Name: VARCHAR(100)

Primary key: Name
Entity name: Model
Attributes:
Model number: CHAR(4)
Model name: VARCHAR(100)
Primary key: Model number

Entity name: Spaceship
Attributes:
Serial number: CHAR(17)
Recommended price: NUMERIC(8, 2)
......

As soon as you see the answer, you may realize that you missed something in formulating your request: naming the entities and attributes properly. The names of entities and attributes don't follow the naming conventions we discussed in chapter 3. To fix that problem, you can ask ChatGPT a follow-up question or reformulate your initial question. Regardless of your choice, we recommend that you give ChatGPT an example of how the output should be formatted. Here is an example follow-up request:

Regenerate your answer using a new format but the same requirements. Make sure that names of entities and attributes are all snake-cased.
New format:
Entity name of Spaceship: spaceship
Attributes:
Serial number: serial_number – CHAR(17)
Recommended price: recommended_price – NUMERIC(8, 2)
Primary key: serial_number

Here is a sample answer from ChatGPT to this request:

ChatGPT GPT-4o

Entity name of Brand: brand
Attributes:
Name: name – VARCHAR(100)
Primary key: name

Entity name of Model: model
Attributes:
Model number: model_number – CHAR(4)
Model name: model_name – VARCHAR(100)
Primary key: model_number

Entity name of Spaceship: spaceship
Attributes:
Serial number: serial_number – CHAR(17)
Recommended price: recommended_price – NUMERIC(8, 2)
Year: year – year
Primary key: serial_number

Entity name of Dealer: dealer
Attributes:
Name: name – VARCHAR(100)
Address: address – VARCHAR(255)
Phone number: phone_number – CHAR(15)
Email address: email_address – VARCHAR(100)
Website URL: website_url – VARCHAR(255)
Primary key: name

Entity name of Customer: `customer`
Attributes:
Name: `name – VARCHAR(100)`
Address: `address – VARCHAR(255)`
Phone number: `phone_number – CHAR(15)`
Email address: `email_address – VARCHAR(100)`
Primary key: `email_address`

As you see, ChatGPT does many things right, such as using the desired format, following snake-case convention in naming entities and attributes, and making some reasonable guesses on data length when no requirements are specified.

Some design choices in the answer are questionable, however. Three notable problems stand out.

First, the selection of primary keys of certain entities may not be what you want. Because the requirement summaries don't provide enough information about how primary keys should be selected, ChatGPT took the liberty of sneaking in some assumptions. The `name` attribute was chosen as the primary key of the `dealer` entity, for example, and the `email_address` attribute was chosen as the primary key of the `customer` entity. Both choices are problematic. Although a dealer's name is not likely to change often, it is possible for two dealers to have the same name, even in a single US state, let alone the world. A different attribute should be used as the primary key, but what would that be? After diving into the requirement analysis further, you find the following information:

- A customer is allowed to update their email address and phone number.
- A dealer is allowed to update their email address and phone number.

In other words, neither the email nor the phone number is stable. If you make either attribute the primary key of an entity, you will face a lot of trouble in updating phone number or email addresses. That said, no single attributes are readily available to be used as the primary key in `dealer` or `customer`. As you learned in chapter 4, a surrogate key that increments automatically can be used as the primary key in this situation. Such a primary key has no problems in identifying a data record uniquely but can't prevent data duplications by itself—that is, it can't prevent a person or a robot to register more than one account using the same information. Based on what you learned in chapter 6, you can add a unique constraint to the `email_address` attribute and another to the `phone_number` attribute to address concerns about data duplication. When you revise the design of the `customer` entity based on these considerations, it looks like this:

Entity name of Customer: `customer`

Attributes:

Customer ID: `customer_id` – INT

Name: `name` – VARCHAR(100)

......

Primary key: `customer_id`

Note 1: `email_address` requires a unique constraint; `phone_number` requires a unique constraint

The `dealer` entity has a similar update:

> **Entity name of Dealer:** `dealer`
>
> **Attributes:**
>
> **Dealer ID:** `dealer_id` – `INT`
>
> **Name:** `name` – `VARCHAR(100)`
>
> ......
>
> **Primary key:** `dealer_id`
>
> ......

Second, the design of phone-number attributes failed to account for the fact that a dealer or customer can be anywhere on Earth. Both `customer` and `dealer` have a `phone_number` attribute. The data length `CHAR(15)` may not be sufficient for all international numbers. If you do some research on phone-number lengths, you find that the maximum length of a phone number is 15 digits, thanks to the international phone-numbering plan. This length assumes that the country code is included and that the number is a simple numeric string without spaces, dashes, or parentheses. Some international numbers, however, have non-numeric strings. In such a case, the total length may exceed 15 characters. To address this problem, you can separate the country code from the phone number and prepare two attributes to store each piece of data separately. When you revise the design of the `customer` entity based on these considerations, it looks like this:

> **Entity name of Customer:** `customer`
>
> **Attributes:**
>
> **Customer ID:** `customer_id` – `INT`
>
> **Name:** `name` – `VARCHAR(100)`
>
> **Phone number:**
>
> ```
>     country_code - CHAR(5)
>     customer_phone_number - CHAR(15)
> ```
>
> ......

The `dealer` entity has a similar update:

Entity name of Dealer: `dealer`

Attributes:

Dealer ID: `dealer_id` – `INT`

Name: `name` – `VARCHAR(100)`

Phone number:

```
country_code - CHAR(5)
dealer_phone_number - CHAR(15)
```

`......`

The separation between country codes and phone numbers can help standardize phone numbers and ensure consistency in how phone numbers are stored. More important, `VARCHAR(15)` is sufficient for any phone numbers when the country code is not considered.

Third, the design of address attributes failed to account for the fact that the dealer and customer can be anywhere on Earth. A single attribute, `VARCHAR(255)`, may not be sufficient for storing some long addresses. What's worse, this design will lead to many addresses with unpredictable formats because no structure is enforced. Unpredictable formats create further troubles in parsing, searching, and filtering, let alone data validation and error handling.

To make address storage more robust and flexible, consider breaking the address into multiple attributes. You might update the design of the `customer` entity like this:

Entity name of Customer: `customer`

Attributes:

`......`

Address:

```
street_address - VARCHAR(255)
suburb - VARCHAR(100)
city - VARCHAR(100)
state_province - VARCHAR(100)
postal_code - VARCHAR(20)
    country - CHAR(2)
```

`......`

The design of the `dealer` entity is updated as follows:

Entity name of Dealer: `dealer`

Attributes:

......

Address:

```
street_address - VARCHAR(255)
  suburb - VARCHAR(100)
  city - VARCHAR(100)
  state_province - VARCHAR(100)
  postal_code - VARCHAR(20)
  country - CHAR(2)
```

......

As soon as you break the address information into six attributes in both the `customer` and `dealer` entities, you may notice that the two entities suddenly have significant overlap. This situation may ring a bell if you remember chapter 7, which addressed a similar problem between a user address and a billing address. If you use the same solution, you can prepare a new table representing addresses and link that table to both the `dealer` and `customer` entities. The new table looks like this:

Entity name of Address: `address`

Attributes:

Address ID: `address_id` - INT

Street address: `street_address` - VARCHAR(255)

Suburb: `suburb` - VARCHAR(100)

City: `city` - VARCHAR(100)

State/Province: `state_province` - VARCHAR(100)

Postal code: `postal_code` - VARCHAR(20)

Country: `country` - CHAR(2)

Primary key: `address_id`

The postal codes are not universally applicable. Some countries use them, and others don't. Countries that use postal codes tend to have different opinions about how they should be formatted. As a result, you should make the `postal_code` attribute optional, which means that it can be `null`. The same can be said of the `suburb` attribute. With the `address` entity representing addresses, you can remove the attributes about addresses from the `customer` and `dealer` entities.

It is important to keep a record of your revisions in text because you are not done designing and implementing the database, and ChatGPT is a primarily a text-based AI tool. You'll feed your design of entities and attributes to ChatGPT again for future design revisions and implementations. When you merge all your revisions with the answers from ChatGPT, you get the following results:

Entity name of Brand: brand
Attributes:
Name: name – VARCHAR(100)
Primary key: name

Entity name of Model: model
Attributes:
Model number: model_number – CHAR(4)
Model name: model_name – VARCHAR(100)
Primary key: model_number

Entity name of Spaceship: spaceship
Attributes:
Serial number: serial_number – CHAR(17)
Recommended price: recommended_price – NUMERIC(8, 2)
Year: year – year
Primary key: serial_number

Entity name of Dealer: dealer
Attributes:
Dealer ID: dealer_id – INT
Name: name – VARCHAR(100)

Email address: `email_address` – `VARCHAR(100)`

Website URL: `website_url` – `VARCHAR(255)`

Phone number:

    `country_code - CHAR(5)`
    `dealer_phone_number - CHAR(15)`

Primary key: `dealer_id`

Note 1: `email_address` requires a unique constraint; (`country_code`, `phone_number`) requires a unique constraint

---

Entity name of Customer: `customer`

Attributes:

Customer ID: `customer_id` – `INT`

Name: `name` – `VARCHAR(100)`

Email address: `email_address` – `VARCHAR(100)`

Phone number:

    `country_code - CHAR(5)`
    `customer_phone_number - CHAR(15)`

Primary key: `customer_id`

Note 1: `email_address` requires a unique constraint; (`country_code`, `phone_number`) requires a unique constraint

---

Entity name of Address: `address`

Attributes:

Address ID: `address_id` – `INT`

Street address: `street_address` – `VARCHAR(255)`

Suburb: `suburb` – `VARCHAR(100)`

City: `city` – `VARCHAR(100)`

State/Province: `state_province` – `VARCHAR(100)`

Postal code: `postal_code` – `VARCHAR(20)`

Country: `country` – `CHAR(2)`

Primary key: `address_id`

Note 1: `suburb` and `postal_code` are optional

Communicate your design

You have completed the design of entities and attributes based on the requirement analysis and ChatGPT. Everything is stored in a long, formatted piece of text. The text is essential for communicating with ChatGPT but not great for sharing your design with other people. To communicate your design effectively, you have to visualize it.

If you have only a few entities, you can use any diagram tool to draw them. You can draw all the entities of SHIPS R US as follows:

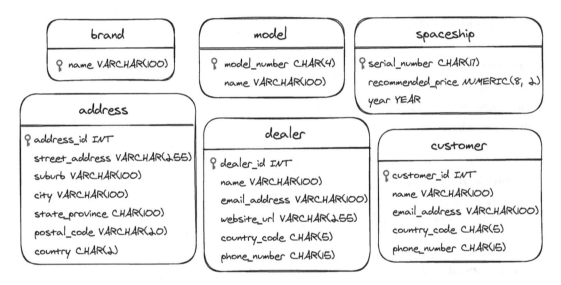

If you are working on a much bigger project that involves a dozen or more entities, however, you may want to turn to ChatGPT for help again. Although ChatGPT can't generate the diagram you need in the target format, you can ask it to generate the corresponding SQL code and import the code into a tool that visualizes database design based on SQL code, such as dbdiagram. io (https://dbdiagram.io). To ask ChatGPT for SQL code, try the following example request:

I am designing a database. Help me generate MySQL code based on the following description of entities and attributes. Keep the entities independent from one another.

Description: """

Entity name of Brand: brand

Attributes:

Name: name – VARCHAR(100)

Primary key: name

......

Country: country – CHAR(2)

Primary key: address_id

Note 1: suburb and postal_code are optional

(This is an excerpt. Full text can be found at https://bit.ly/grdb.)

"""

After getting the code, you can copy and paste it by using the import function of dbdiagram.io:

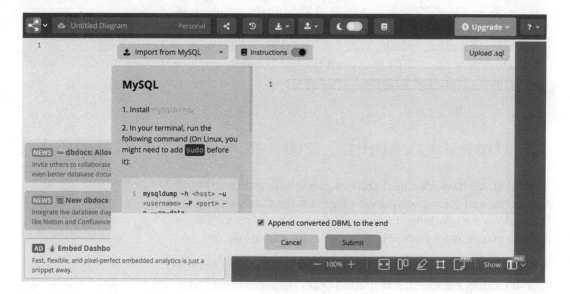

The generated visualization is much easier to share with others and appropriate for communication:

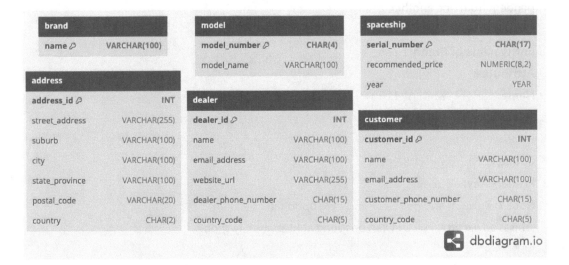

As you can see, ChatGPT can speed the process of database design. Although you can't use the answers directly, they are useful as the starting point in your problem-solving journey. When you get some answers from ChatGPT, it is up to you to identify the problems in those answers and fix them based on your requirement analysis and knowledge of database design. When you need to communicate your design to others, ChatGPT can convert the text-based design to SQL code, which in turn can be turned into a diagram.

Relationships among entities

Now that you have identified and designed all the entities, their attributes, and corresponding data types for the database, you are ready to work on the relationships among entities. The following list may refresh your memory of the requirements for relationships:

- The database needs to maintain records of all spaceship brands and models, manufactured spaceships, dealers, customers, and relationships between dealers and customers.

- A spaceship brand is associated with multiple models, and a model is associated with multiple spacecraft.
- A dealer is distributed one or more spaceships and serves one or more customers.
- A customer is served by one or more dealer, and is associated with one or more spaceships that they bought from the dealer.
- A spaceship is associated with one model and can be associated with no more than one owner and no more than one dealer.
- A customer is associated with one address. Multiple customers may share an address. A dealer is associated with one address.

You added the last item when you decided to use an independent entity to represent addresses. You need to address the relationship between customers and addresses as you build the relationships among entities; the same is true of dealers and addresses.

As what you did in the preceding section, you can start by asking ChatGPT to generate a design draft. To achieve a more useful response, follow the rules of thumb to structure your request. Try the following request:

I am designing a database for a manufacturer of spaceships. I have identified six entities: brand, model, spaceship, dealer, customer, and address. Help me identify the relationships between each pair of entities based on the given requirements. Generate output using the desired format.

Desired format:

brand | model

Relationship: one to many

Note: The side pointing to model is many

Requirements: " " "

The database needs to maintain records of all spaceship brands and models ...... A dealer is associated with one address.

(This is an excerpt. Full text can be found at https://bit.ly/grdb.)

" " "

Here is a sample response from ChatGPT:

ChatGPT GPT-4o

brand | model
Relationship: one to many
Note: the side pointing to model is many

model | spaceship
Relationship: one to many
Note: The side pointing to spaceship is many

spaceship | dealer
Relationship: many to one
Note: The side pointing to dealer is one

spaceship | customer
Relationship: many to one
Note: A customer can own multiple spaceships, and a spaceship can be owned by multiple customers (e.g., shared ownership)

dealer | address
Relationship: one to one
Note: Each dealer is associated with exactly one address

customer | address
Relationship: many to one
Note: The side pointing to address is one

As in the design of entities and attributes, ChatGPT does many things right. In the preceding answer, most relationships were developed properly with the exception of the relationship between customer and spaceship. The requirements you gathered were quite explicit:

A customer is served by a
dealer and is associated with
one or more spaceships that
they bought.

A customer is associated
with one or more spaceships.

A spaceship is associated
with one model and can be
associated with no more than
one owner and no more than
one dealer.

A spaceship is associated
with up to one owner.

It is possible that when the information on a relationship is scattered across multiple sentences, ChatGPT has difficulty parsing it properly. It is also possible that ChatGPT somehow starts to hallucinate when answering this question. Regardless, you have a robust mastery of database design after reading the first seven chapters of this book, and the error is not hard to fix:

spaceship | customer
Relationship: many to one
Note: the side pointing to customer is one

You may also notice that the relationship between customer and dealer is missing. The requirement you gathered is clear:

- A dealer serves one or more customers.
- A customer is served by a dealer.

You can add this relationship yourself to the text of relationships:

customer | dealer
Relationship: many to many
Note: both sides are many

Minimum cardinalities and foreign keys

ChatGPT didn't provide much information about the min cardinalities or foreign keys of relationships between pairs of entities. You didn't ask for this information to begin with because you needed to make sure that each relationship (max cardinalities) was identified properly first. Now is a good time to make a new request to ChatGPT. Here is an example of how you might structure this request:

I am designing a database for a manufacturer of spaceships. I have identified some of the characteristics of six entities: brand, model, spaceship, dealer, customer, and address. Help me identify the min cardinality and where the foreign key should be placed between each pair of entities based on the given requirements and the known relationship characteristics. Generate output using the desired format.

Desired format:

brand | model

Relationship: one to many

Note 1: The side pointing to model is many

Note 2: The foreign is in model

Note 3: The min cardinality close to model is relaxed from 1 to 0

Requirements: """

The database needs to maintain records of all spaceship brands and models ...... A dealer is associated with one address.

(This is an excerpt. Full text can be found at https://bit.ly/grdb.)

"""

Characteristics: """

brand | model

Relationship: one to many

Note: The side pointing to model is many

......

customer | address

Relationship: many to one

Note: The side pointing to address is one

(This is an excerpt. Full text can be found at https://bit.ly/grdb.)

"""

Following is a sample answer from ChatGPT to this request:

ChatGPT GPT-4o

brand | model

Relationship: one to many

Note 1: The side pointing to model is many

Note 2: The foreign key is in model

Note 3: The minimum cardinality close to model is relaxed from 1 to 0

model | spaceship

Relationship: one to many

Note 1: The side pointing to spaceship is many

Note 2: The foreign key is in spaceship

Note 3: The minimum cardinality close to spaceship is relaxed from 1 to 0

customer | dealer

Relationship: many to many

Note 1: A junction table `customer_dealer` is needed

Note 2: The foreign keys are in `customer_dealer`

Note 3: The minimum cardinalities close to `customer_dealer` are relaxed from 1 to 0

spaceship | dealer

Relationship: many to one

Note 1: The side pointing to dealer is one

Note 2: The foreign key is in spaceship

Note 3: The minimum cardinality close to dealer is relaxed from 1 to 0

spaceship | customer

Relationship: many to one

Note 1: The side pointing to customer is one

Note 2: The foreign key is in spaceship

Note 3: The minimum cardinality close to spaceship is relaxed from 1 to 0

*(**continued**)*

dealer | address

Relationship: one to one

Note 1: Each dealer is associated with exactly one address

Note 2: The foreign key is in dealer

Note 3: The minimum cardinality close to address is 1

customer | address

Relationship: many to one

Note 1: The side pointing to address is one

Note 2: The foreign key is in customer

Note 3: The minimum cardinality close to address is relaxed from 1 to 0

ChatGPT handled the placement of foreign keys quite well, especially when three entities are related. The relationships among `customer`, `dealer`, and `address` are similar to a challenge you tackled in earlier chapters: how to handle the relationships among address, user, and payment methods for The Sci-Fi Collective. The relationships among `customer`, `dealer`, and `address` are summarized as follows:

Beyond foreign keys, ChatGPT is rather confused about the min cardinalities, especially when a min cardinality needs to be relaxed from one to zero. It is up to you to fix those mistakes, using what you learned from chapter 5. If your memory is blurred, here are some rules of thumb about when to relax a min cardinality:

- In a one-to-one relationship, if one entity is typically created before the other, you may set the min cardinality of the second entity to zero to allow the first entity to exist without an immediate counterpart.

- In a one-to-many relationship, the cardinality that's closer to the many side needs to be relaxed. This relaxation allows for cases in which the entity on the one side might exist without any corresponding entries on the many side. A customer might exist without any addresses, for example.
- In a many-to-many relationship, the min cardinalities are often set to zero on both sides if either entity can exist without the other. If there are strict business rules about the existence of the entities, however, you might keep one cardinality set to one.

You can start with the relationships between `dealer` and `address` and between `customer` and `address`. The gathered requirements don't say much about the min cardinalities of their relationships. After following up with the software developers, you gained some new understanding:

- *A dealer can't have an account without an address.* SHIPS R US's web app doesn't allow dealers to register accounts without providing address information. In other words, it is not possible for a dealer record to exist without a corresponding address.
- *SHIPS R US maintains user records for purposes such as outreach and recalls but doesn't allow customers to register accounts directly.* Instead, dealers enter the customer information plus the address information into the system. In other words, it is not possible for a customer record to exist without a corresponding address.

Combining such information and rules of thumb about when to relax a min cardinality, you can make the following revisions:

customer | address   *The min cardinality close to customer is relaxed from 1 to 0*
Relationship: many to one
Note 1: The side pointing to address is one
Note 2: The foreign key is in customer
Note 3: ~~The minimum cardinality close to address is relaxed from 1 to 0~~

dealer | address   *The min cardinality close to dealer is relaxed from 1 to 0*
Relationship: one to one
Note 1: Each dealer is associated with exactly one address Note 2: The foreign key is in dealer
Note 3: ~~The minimum cardinality close to address is 1~~

The revision to the relationship between `customer` and `address` is straightforward considering that the relationship is one-to-many. The min cardinality of the many side needs to be relaxed to make data entry possible. By contrast, the revision to the relationship between `dealer` and `address` is more nuanced. You may wonder whether you can relax the side closer to `address` instead of `dealer`. You can, but doing so will make things messier and less consistent, as demonstrated in the following figure:

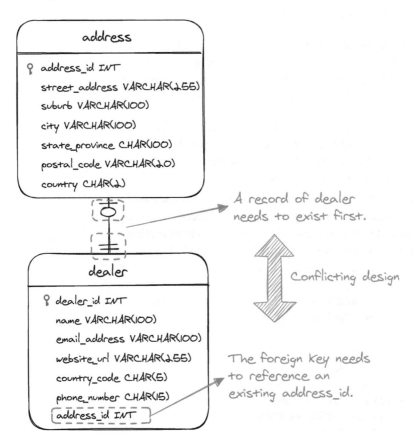

Because `dealer` is the child table in this relationship, it contains the foreign key `address_id`. In other words, a new record in the `dealer` table needs to reference an existing `address_id` value. As the result, relaxing the cardinality closer to `dealer` is a better choice. The revised relationships between `customer` and `address` and between `dealer` and `address` can be summarized as follows:

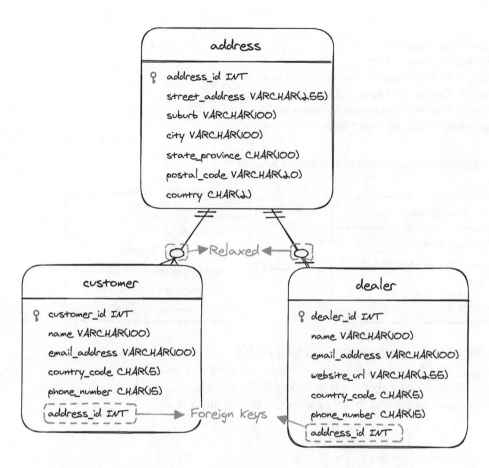

Beyond the two relationships, you can find one more min cardinalities that need to be relaxed in the relationship between `spaceship` and `customer`. The requirements for this relationship are

- A spaceship is associated with one model and can be associated with no more than one owner and no more than one dealer.
- A customer is associated with one or more spaceships that they bought.

In other words, when a spaceship is manufactured, its record is entered into the system immediately without being associated with a customer. Based on this information, the min cardinality close to `customer` rather than `spaceship` needs to be relaxed to zero:

spaceship | customer   *The min cardinality close to*
                          customer is relaxed from 1 to 0
Relationship: many to one
Note 1: The side pointing to customer is one
Note 2: The foreign key is in spaceship
Note 3: ~~The minimum cardinality close to spaceship is relaxed from 1 to 0~~

The revised relationship can be summarized as follows:

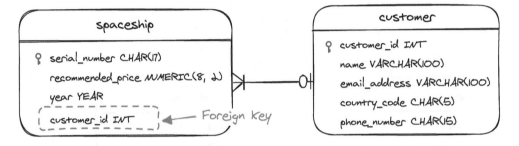

You may notice that the foreign key of this relationship (`customer_id`) is in `spaceship`. By default, `customer_id` needs to reference a record in `customer`. To make sure that the foreign key is aligned with the requirements, make it optional. In other words, it should allow `NULL` values.

Communicate your design

As discussed earlier in this chapter in the "Entities and attributes" section, you are likely to need visualization to communicate your design better. If you choose to draw your design by hand, you'll get something like the following figure.

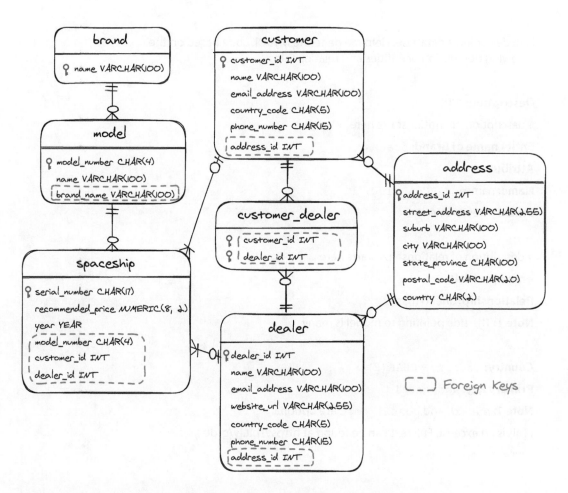

If you need ChatGPT and dbdigram.io for a much bigger project, you must retrieve the SQL code first. The following request aims to get MySQL code from ChatGPT:

I am designing a database. Help me generate MySQL code based on the following description of entities and relationships.

Description: """
description of entities starts here
Entity name of Brand: `brand`
Attributes:
Name: name – `VARCHAR(100)`
Primary key: name

……
description of relationships starts here
brand | model
Relationship: one to many
Note 1: The side pointing to model is many

……
Country: `country` – `CHAR(2)`
Primary key: `address_id`
Note 1: `suburb` and `postal_code` are optional
(This is an excerpt. Full text can be found at https://bit.ly/grdb.)
"""

After getting the code, you can copy and paste it into dbdiagram.io to get the following diagram:

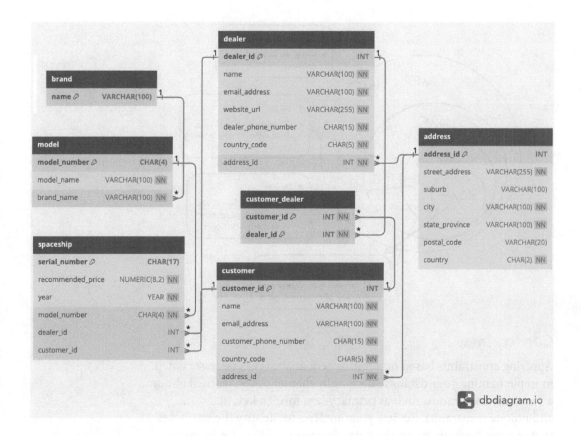

Implementation

Now that you designed the entities, attributes, and relationships for the database of SHIPS R US, you are ready to implement the database. First, however, you have to make sure that your database design is normalized. When you check your database design against the requirements for normal forms, you see that your database design is in Boyce-Codd Normal Form (BCNF). You can also ask ChatGPT to help with the checking ("Is my database design normalized?") and verify the answers later.

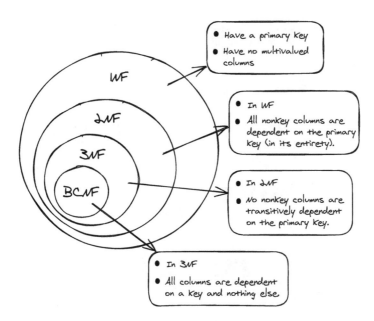

Constraints

Applying constraints based on requirement analysis is a necessary step in implementing your database design. In chapter 6, you learned about a variety of constraints, such as primary key, foreign key, NOT NULL, and unique constraints. Review your analysis to identify the attributes that require constraints and the type of constraints that are appropriate. ChatGPT can offer help for this task as well. Copy and paste all the relevant requirements and the revised output from the preceding two sections and then formulate a new request:

> I am designing a database. Help me identify the attributes that need constraints and the type of constraints using the desired format based on the given requirements, entities and attributes, and relationships among entities.
>
> **Desired formats:**
>
> **Entity name:** brand
>
> **Attribute in focus:**
>
> * model_number: primary key
>
> * model_name: NOT NULL
>
> * brand_name: foreign key

Requirements: """
The database needs to maintain records of all spaceship brands and models, manufactured ......
(This is an excerpt. Full text can be found at https://bit.ly/grdb.)
"""

Entity and attributes: """
Entity name of Brand: `brand`
Attributes:
Name: `name – VARCHAR(100)` ......
(This is an excerpt. Full text can be found at https://bit.ly/grdb.)
"""

Relationships: """
brand | model
Relationship: one to many
Note 1: The side pointing to model is many......
(This is an excerpt. Full text can be found at https://bit.ly/grdb.)
"""

Here is a sample answer to this request:

ChatGPT GPT-4o

Entity: `Brand`
Attribute in focus:
name: primary key

Entity: `Model`
Attributes in focus:
`model_number`: primary key constraint
`model_name`: NOT NULL
`brand_name`: foreign key constraint (references `brand.name`)

(*continued*)

Entity: Spaceship
Attributes in focus:

serial_number: primary key

recommended_price: CHECK (e.g., CHECK (recommended_price >= 0))

year: CHECK (e.g., CHECK (year >= 1900))

model_number: foreign key (references model.model_number)

dealer_id: foreign key (references dealer.dealer_id)

customer_id: foreign key (references customer.customer_id)

Entity: Dealer
Attributes in focus:

dealer_id: primary key

name: NOT NULL

email_address: UNIQUE

website_url: NOT NULL

(country_code, dealer_phone_number): UNIQUE

address_id: foreign key (references address.address_id)

Entity: Customer
Attributes in focus:

customer_id: primary key

name: NOT NULL

email_address: UNIQUE

(country_code, customer_phone_number): UNIQUE

address_id: foreign key (references address.address_id)

Entity: Customer_Dealer
Attributes in focus:

(customer_id, dealer_id): primary key

customer_id: foreign key (references customer.customer_id)

dealer_id: foreign key (references dealer.dealer_id)

> **Entity:** Address
>
> **Attributes in focus:**
>
> address_id: primary key
>
> country: CHECK (ensures valid country codes, e.g., CHECK (country IN ('US', 'CA', ...)))

As you see, ChatGPT properly identified most of the constraints, but it missed a few attributes that require NOT NULL constraints. Also, it neglected the scenarios in which an attribute requires more than one constraint. email_address in dealer, for example, requires both NOT NULL and UNIQUE constraints. You need to fix these problems yourself and store revised text of the constraints so that you can use them for the next step.

Optimization

In optimization, you aim to reduce redundancy and increase the consistency and efficiency of your database design before converting it to code. You can pose some open-ended general questions to ChatGPT (such as "How do I optimize my database design?"). But asking specific questions about certain things that you notice always results in better responses.

You may notice, for example, that the ChatGPT suggested using a CHECK constraint on the `country` attribute in `address`. Considering that there are about 200 countries in the world, however, this constraint will be painful to code and messy. You can raise a question about this aspect:

> Q1. Applying a CHECK constraint to the `country` attribute in the address table is painful because there are about 200 countries in the world. What's a common and recommended approach to store such information without this constraint but still retain the data validity check?

You can raise the same question about the `country_code` attribute in `customer` and `dealer`:

> Q2. To ensure the validity of the country code of phone numbers in the `customer/address` tables, what's a common and recommended approach to store such information?

ChatGPT's responses are quite useful:

> ## ChatGPT GPT-4o
>
> Q1 Answer: Instead of using a CHECK constraint for the country code, a better approach is to use a reference to a separate `Country` table. This table would contain a list of valid country codes and their corresponding names ...
>
> Q2 Answer: To ensure the data validity, you can follow a similar approach to use a separate table ...

To synthesize the two suggestions, you can create a single table to store information about each country, such as country abbreviation, country code, and name. The table will be prepopulated with valid information, so it can be linked to `customer`, `dealer`, and `address` to ensure data validity. The updated database design is as follows:

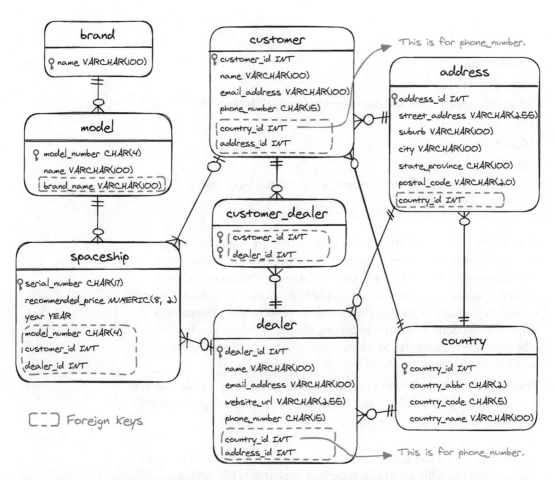

You need to update the information you stored about entities, attributes, relationships, and constraints. Then you will be ready to convert the updated design to SQL code with the help of ChatGPT. To achieve the best result, be specific in your request. Here is an example request that asks for MySQL code:

I am designing a database. Generate MySQL code based on the given entity, attributes, and relationships, and constraints.
Entity and attributes: """
Entity name of Brand: brand ......
(This is an excerpt. Full text can be found at https://bit.ly/grdb.)
"""

(*continued*)

Relationships: " " "

brand | model ......

(This is an excerpt. Full text can be found at https://bit.ly/grdb.)

" " "

Constraints: " " "

Entity: brand ......

(This is an excerpt. Full text can be found at https://bit.ly/grdb.)

" " "

Depending on the RDBMS you are using, you may want the code to be in a different SQL dialect. As long as the provided information is detailed enough, it is hard for ChatGPT to make serious mistakes at this step. You can find the full SQL code in `chapter_08` folder in our GitHub repository. If your requirements have sufficient information about which columns require indexing, chapter 7 shows you how to take preemptive measures to index those columns. Otherwise, you can wait for the data and the use of database tell you more.

Finally, ChatGPT can be very useful for generating sample data that you can use to test your database and for identifying problems preemptively. Following is a sample request for testing data:

I am designing a database. Generate sample data that can be used for testing based on the given SQL code that implements the database.

SQL Code:

```
'''
-- Create brand table
CREATE TABLE brand (name VARCHAR(100) PRIMARY KEY);
......
-- Create customer_dealer table
CREATE TABLE customer_dealer (
   customer_id INT NOT NULL,
   dealer_id INT NOT NULL,
   CONSTRAINT pk_customer_dealer ......
   CONSTRAINT fk_customer_dealer_customer ......
   CONSTRAINT fk_customer_dealer_dealer ......
);
```

(This is a snippet. Full code can be found at https://bit.ly/grdb.)

" " "

Now you've gone through the full process of database design with the help of ChatGPT. Good job!

Recap

- To use ChatGPT for database design effectively, follow some rules of thumb: be specific, descriptive, and as detailed as possible; separate instructions from context; and articulate the desired output format through examples.
- You should take a stepwise approach to using ChatGPT to help with database design and make verifications and revisions to ChatGPT's output at each step.
- Store the design at each milestone in text for smooth communication with ChatGPT in the future.
- If you need to communicate your design draft with coworkers, you can convert your design to SQL code with the help of ChatGPT and visualize it by using tools such as dbdiagram.io.

index